Martin Luther King, Jr.

Martin Luther King, Jr.

Ron Ramdin

HAUS PUBLISHING • LONDON

First published in Great Britain in 2004 by
Haus Publishing Limited
26 Cadogan Court, Draycott Avenue
London SW3 3BX

Copyright ©Ron Ramdin 2004

The moral right of the authors has been asserted

A CIP catalogue record for this book is available from the British Library

ISBN 1-904341-82-9

Designed and typeset in Garamond
Printed and bound by Antony Rowe Ltd, Chippenham, Wiltshire

Front cover: photograph courtesy of Akg-Images
Back cover: photograph courtesy of Getty Images

CONDITIONS OF SALE
All rights reserved. No part of this publication may be reproduced, stored in a retrieval system, or transmitted in any form or by any means, electronic, mechanical, photocopying, recording or otherwise, without the prior permission of the publisher

This book is sold subject to the condition that it shall not, by way of trade or otherwise, be lent, re-sold, hired out or otherwise circulated without the publisher's prior consent in any form of binding or cover other than that in which it is published and without a similar condition including this condition being imposed on the subsequent purchaser

Contents

Introduction	1
Early Life	6
Morehouse College and Crozer Seminary	11
Boston University	20
Montgomery's moment of truth	29
Beyond Montgomery	44
Journey to India	52
Sit-ins and politics	58
From Albany to Birmingham	64
The 'dream' and the reality	80
Protest, the 'Prize' and Malcolm X	88
SCLC campaigns and black power	101
Vietnam and the Poor People's Campaign	114
Memphis farewell	119
Notes	123
Chronology	128
Further Reading	136
Picture Sources	146
Index	147

I say to you today, my friends, that in spite of the difficulties and frustrations of the moment I still have a dream. It is a dream deeply rooted in the American dream. I have a dream that one day this nation will rise up and live out the true meaning of its creed. We hold these truths to be self-evident: that all men are created equal.
Martin Luther King, Jr
Speech delivered at the Lincoln Memorial at the March on Washington, 28 August 1963

We must accept finite disappointment, but we must never lose infinite hope.
Martin Luther King, Jr
In My Own Words

Introduction

Martin Luther King, Jr. was the second born, the first son of proud parents who were thankful and overjoyed when he arrived. But at the time of his birth on 15 January 1929, there was nothing in his family background to suggest he would become a man so extraordinary that he would join the pantheon of great Americans. Who was he? How did he become one of the makers of the 20th century?

The year of his birth coincided with the onset of the Great Depression of the 1930s that had far-reaching consequences. African-Americans were especially affected and this fact is all the more interesting in considering his family history and the early years of his life.

Whichever side of his family we look at, both were profoundly affected by the events that followed Emancipation in the United States in 1865. Being legally free had naturally aroused great hopes among African-Americans in the post-slavery reconstruction that was undertaken by the Republican Party, whose 'experiment' aimed to establish political and social equality. But white Southerners (among them former slave owners) mounted strong opposition, using intimidation and violence to maintain control over African-Americans. Just over a decade after the slaves became free in law, the Republican Party decided to halt its 'experiment,' thus betraying the freed men and women who were now left to deal with former slave masters and other oppressors, as best they could.[1]

In the ensuing years, segregation in the South had restricted, at every level, relations between white and black Americans. By the First World War, race and colour had underscored a system that perceived African-Americans as inferior and, therefore, excluded from enjoying their basic rights as free people. Even the 'Negro' schools and colleges were limited to education relating to 'menial' (industrial, domestic and agricultural) occupations in keeping with the prevalent view that educating 'a nigger' meant spoiling 'a good field hand'. This attitude, designed to keep African-Americans 'in their place', was at the core of the white supremacist system, within which the majority of African-Americans were 'sharecroppers' and landless labourers. The rigidity of this segregation created unbearable frustrations and tensions. The desire among the oppressed to escape was intense and ever-present, for it was a brutal system. It is said that between 1900 and 1929, white men had lynched 1,641 black men and in 1906 African-Americans in Atlanta were the victims of white mob violence in one of the South's worst race riots. Ironically, Atlanta was also the base of the modern Ku Klux Klan.[2] These were hard times.

> The Ku Klux Klan (KKK) was a racist organisation of white supremacists. Its second incarnation emerged in 1915, out of a nostalgia for the Old South, a wider fear of communism and, most important, the changing ethnic make-up of US society. Its members violently fought the civil rights movement using whippings, lynchings, bombings and shootings. Today, its influence is marginal.

Little Martin was first named Michael after his father, who had later changed both their names to Martin Luther. As he grew up, Martin's siblings were sister Christine, who was older than him and brother Alfred Daniel.

King, Sr, was the son of a sharecropper who lived in Stockbridge, Georgia, some 18 miles from Atlanta. He was so upset one day on the plantation where his father worked that he decided to leave the farm. The incident that sparked-off his departure related to his father being cheated of his earnings. Unable to contain his anger, he spoke out on his father's behalf. The plantation boss was not pleased and threatened to slap the teenager down if his father couldn't deal with him. This experience and dim prospects in the neighbourhood propelled the young man away from Stockbridge.

He left preoccupied with educating himself. He had little schooling and was 18 years old when he arrived in Atlanta. After finishing high school he attended Morehouse College. Later, he displayed great energy and zeal as a preacher. He was ambitious, his eye on the big chance for social and economic advancement. Soon, he was courting the daughter of the highly respected pastor of Atlanta's Ebenezer Baptist Church, the Rev A D Williams. On 25 November 1926, he married Alberta Williams.[3]

Martin Jr would later recall that the thing he most admired about his father was his unswerving Christian character, integrity, commitment to moral and ethical principles and conscientiousness. He also said his father's directness in speaking the truth had *caused people to fear him*. And not surprisingly, this energetic, principled man, possessed of leadership qualities was involved in civil rights through the National Association for the Advancement of Coloured People (NAACP). So the question of 'Jim Crow' segregation in Atlanta had been an ongoing issue for King Sr, who had set a precedent for those to come by refusing to use the city's buses after he had seen a violent attack on black passengers. He was also at the

The term 'Jim Crow' originated in the early 19th century, when Thomas "Daddy" Rice, a white entertainer, blackened his face with charcoal paste or burnt cork and danced a jig to the song, Jump Jim Crow. By the 20th century, it had evolved into both a derogatory description of African-Americans and was used as a moniker for the prevailing system of segregation.

The Rev Martin Luther King Snr (second left) protesting against segregated buses 1957

forefront of the struggle in Atlanta to get equal pay for teachers and helped to abolish Jim Crow elevators in the Courthouse.

These activities did not deflect 'Daddy' King, as Martin called his father, from his fatherly responsibilities, which he shouldered in exemplary fashion. Martin and the rest of the family were never short of food and clothing. Neither did they want for adequate shelter.[4] Why? Because Daddy did not live beyond his means. His economic good sense, however, came with strict and even harsh, discipline. But this should not obscure what Martin recognised as the warmth that characterised relations within the King family.

Throughout his life Martin exhibited unabashed respect and affection for his father. In a revealing essay written when he was 20 years old, King praised his father as a *real father* – someone who *always placed his family first*. Glossing over the fact that his father had married into wealth, Martin stressed Daddy's capacity for hard work and frugality, which he had experienced and learned well in his early life. *He never wastes his money at the expense of his family*, King wrote. He was always careful to live within his means. And despite his father's discipline, King never forgot the comforting, intimate relationships of the King household.[5]

King Sr's influence upon his son, could also be understood in terms of his bourgeois inclination. While the economic depression and poverty tore black families apart, Daddy was able to meet all his family's needs. He was also clearly the exception to the rule; and Martin felt guilty about his good fortune in having such a father.

Put simply, his Daddy showed him the way. *I guess the influence of my father had a great deal to do with my going into the Ministry, he confessed. My admiration for him was a great moving factor, he set forth a noble example I didn't mind following.*[6]

Martin's mother Alberta was also deeply religious. But unlike her husband, she spoke softly. She was easy going, with an unshowy personality that was nonetheless warm and approachable.

This daughter of the Rev Williams was an only child who grew up in relative comfort. But the pleasant upbringing she had enjoyed and the protection she received from the 'worst blights' of discrimination were not enough to help her to adjust to Jim Crow, which she deeply abhorred. Amid this rancorous, demeaning atmosphere, she did all she could to instil self-respect in her children. Every African-American parent had to confront the problem of, as King later put it, *how to explain discrimination and segregation to a small child*. Although she taught Martin to feel a 'sense of somebodiness'[7] and encouraged him to feel worthy, equal to other (meaning white) people, she drew his attention to slavery and the American Civil War and explained the 'divided' (and divisive) system in the South which affected schools, cafes, restaurant, theatres, housing, waiting rooms and lavatories. She left her son in no doubt about the depth of feeling against the system and impressed upon him that he 'must never allow it to make him feel inferior'. He was 'as good as anyone', she said. Little Martin never forgot those motherly words.

Early life

Martin Luther King, Jr was born at 501 Auburn Avenue where Atlanta's main black businesses were located. Here the Ebenezer Church stood, an imposing and symbolic landmark of the black community with a congregation of many thousands. Cocooned within the security of his family, King grew up conscious of his lineage as the grandson and son of Baptist preachers.[8] Church life was life as he knew it. Although he was too young to understand what was happening during the Depression, by about the age of five, young Martin was already questioning his parents about the people he saw queuing for bread. His family didn't. Why?

He was intelligent, alert, a quick learner, unafraid to follow others. When his sister Christine had joined the church, he felt he should do likewise. Later, he explained that he followed her not out of any dynamic conviction, but out of a childhood desire to keep up with her. His relationship with the Church was far more involved than this. Regardless of what he felt about joining, there was an inevitability about the fact that the church (especially since his father had taken over the pastorate of Ebenezer when Rev Williams died) became his second home. Because religious life was his birthright and early experience, he had not experienced the 'crisis moment' of conversion to Christianity. For him, this was the thing to do. He had no choice but to live amidst the trappings of strong faith, of prayer meetings, community socials, revivals, music and talk of the black church and the black community. If all this seemed excessive, he later dispelled any doubts by saying he *never regretted* going to church.[9]

In these early years he was taught the fundamentalist line of Christianity and accepted his teacher's belief in the infallibility of the Scriptures. He said most of those who instructed him were *unlettered* men, whose authority was unchallenged. In fact, Biblical criticism was unheard of, especially from minors. He felt no need to doubt these godly men until he was about 12 years old. This was a critical juncture in Martin's life for he says that accepting things uncritically was contrary to his nature. But as a 'precocious type' the time for questioning soon began. He shocked his classmates at Sunday school when he questioned the resurrection of Christ. Thereafter, doubts about aspects of religion became integral to this thinking.

In late childhood and early adolescence, he identified two incidents which he admitted had largely affected his development. First, was the loss of his grandmother, whose death had evoked in him nostalgic thoughts of being her 'favourite grandchild.' In turn, he expressed his 'extreme love' for her. The suddenness and finality of her death stunned him and soon after, as he later recalled, his parents tried to explain to him the doctrine of immortality. They assured him, and he believed them, that his grandmother 'still lived'. He was beginning to accept that there is no finality in death and this is why, he later declared his belief in 'personal immortality'.

The second incident occurred at about the age of six. Earlier, from the time he was three, he and his best playmate, a white boy, played games with abandon. Then when they were six, they were separated; each attended a different school and soon their friendship ended because the white boy's father forbade its continuation. This sudden closure of friendship was upsetting. Naturally, he sought help. Surely, he would meet his friend again; he thought an explanation was needed. It was in the ensuing discussion with his parents that he first became aware of a 'race problem' and the 'tragedies' that resulted from it.

The shock of separation electrified him, causing at first confusion, then rage. *From that moment on*, he said, *I was determined to hate every white person*, a feeling that persisted as he grew older. As a counterpoise, his god-fearing parents insisted that instead of hating white people, it was his Christian duty to love them. *How could he? How could I love a race of people who hated me and who had been responsible for breaking me up with one of my best childhood friends?* This question would trouble him for years.

Soon his growing concern brought him up against the 'system'. He remembered visiting a store with his father when a young white assistant asked them to remove themselves from the seats they had occupied at the front of the store to seats at the back. Martin was surprised, his father responded immediately, saying he was comfortable where he was. The store assistant was incensed and insisted that the prospective buyers should move as he had suggested. At this stage, Daddy King had had enough. If he couldn't buy shoes where he sat, he would rather buy none. There was momentary stalemate and eventually father and son left the store. If he had any doubts, the experience taught young Martin the revealing, fundamental lesson that the segregated system under which they lived was non-negotiable to both his father and mother.

On another occasion, Daddy was again forthright in his response, this time to being called 'boy' by a white policeman, a word which Daddy pretended he had not heard. He stood his ground. His uncompromising behaviour had shocked the policeman who got the message and beat a hasty retreat.[10]

Nonetheless, there was little or no room for flexibility in segregated Atlanta. African-Americans were also denied access to public places, including swimming pools, public walkways, public parks, white schools and stores.

And some years earlier when he was eight, an incident resulted in him receiving a slap from a white woman who alleged that he had stepped on her foot. He knew well the penalty for reacting to such provocation. But this was not the reason why he did not retaliate. In later years, he explained: *I think some of it was part of my native structure*. It was, however, his bus experience while at Booker T Washington High School that made him think more deeply about the segregated seating arrangements: whites in front, African-Americans confined to the rear, even if there were empty seats in the white section. Often he would walk to the back of the bus, but each time he did so, his mind was centred on the vacated front seat. What he wished for most was that one day he would be able to put his body where his mind was.[11]

Instead of the improvement Martin had hoped for, worse was to follow. Teenagehood had arrived and at the age of 14 he felt the 'angriest' in his life. He had travelled back to Atlanta with his teacher, Ms Bradley, who had gone with him to Dublin, Georgia to participate in an oratorical contest which he won. His euphoria was, however, quickly dampened on the bus. At a certain stage on the journey back, when some white passengers had boarded the bus the white driver ordered Martin and Ms Bradley to vacate their seats and move to the rear so that the incoming people could be seated. The driver cursed Martin who was determined to stay in his seat until Ms Bradley urged him to give it up. She said they had to respect the law; and so reluctantly Martin and Ms Bradley stood at the back of the bus for some 90 miles, each of which rankled deeply within him. He would never forget that night.[12]

So, well into his teens, King had been learning more and more about segregation. Importantly, he learned that the flip side of the coin of racial injustice was economic injustice. Precocious and sensitive, he was highly attuned to the discrepancies that surrounded him in Atlanta and life in the relative economic security and comfort at home. He could not come to terms with the 'tragic poverty' of many children and people in the neighbourhood. He was troubled, too, about the exploitation of poor whites, which he viewed as another aspect of injustice.

Summertime labour on a tobacco farm in Simsbury, Connecticut was instructive. It was his first experience of being away from the protected world of home, the Church and community and the first time that he was plunged into the world of work. He saw and experienced many things that surprised him, especially the absence of discrimination among the white people he had met. It took a while for him to get used to the idea that he could go anywhere and sit anywhere and move around so freely. He ate in one of Hartford's finest restaurants. Much too soon though this sense of freedom gave way to the familiar, rancorous feeling reactivated by his return to segregation.[13]

Overall, these experiences of Martin's childhood and early teens added up. Thus far his schooling had made him aware of local and national issues and importantly, his elaboration of 'The Negro and the Constitution', the theme of his prize-winning speech. His changing, youthful voice echoed a maturity beyond his years. The precocious youth had all along been learning through observation and now he articulated thoughts about the relationship between the economic, the religious and the political. Finally, he concluded his oratory by reminding his audience of the millions of his forebears who had ceaselessly tried to translate the Thirteenth, Fourteenth and Fifteenth Amendments into action. Freedom should not be partial, it should be unqualified for all.[14]

Morehouse College and Crozer Seminary

By his mid-teens, young Martin was full of doubt and began to question certain beliefs which his father held.[15] But, he realised, there was much to learn. When on 20 September 1944, at the age of 15, King, Jr, began his freshman year at the prestigious Morehouse College in Atlanta, he was following in the footsteps of his father and maternal grandfather. He was among the youngest, 'a pretty young fellow' at Morehouse, where he felt much excitement, all the more because the relaxed atmosphere was conducive to the study and discussion of race and racial troubles. Already concerned with economic inequities, for the first time, he came to know about the theory of non-violent resistance through his reading of Henry David Thoreau's essay, 'On Civil Disobedience'. This essay which, in essence, concerned non-cooperation with an 'evil system' won King's attention to the extent that he read the work repeatedly. He was convinced of the moral obligation of seeing the direct relevance of Thoreau's teachings to civil rights concerns.[16]

Henry David Thoreau (1817–62) a writer, philosopher and naturalist, is best known for his essay, 'On Civil Disobedience'. Written after he spent a night in jail for refusing to pay his poll tax – a protest against slavery and war with Mexico – the treatise explained how civil disobedience by the individual citizen was an effective protest against unjust governance. The text was important in inspiring the non-violent philosophies of Mahatma Gandhi and, later, Martin Luther King, Jr.

How to make racial justice a reality was a question that preoccupied many students at Morehouse and few more so than Martin who kept away from members of the 'white race', until he met and associated with white people who were 'allies'. With time, his resentment was replaced by a 'spirit of co-operation', and he worked with existing organisations. He had reached the point where he became deeply concerned with politics and society. And interestingly, he was sufficiently imbued with the spirit of Morehouse to see himself as contributing to the removal of legal barriers to the rights of African-Americans.[17]

While fellow students were confident about their calling in life, at this time, King still kept an open mind. What was clear though was his sense of responsibility towards his fellow men. But even this urge, he thought, was inadequate because it could 'probably' be better satisfied by him being either a lawyer or doctor. Alternatively, he could, of course, turn to the Church in which he had already been assisting his father.

Gradually, the doubts that beset him at this time had the positive effect of freeing him from fundamentalism and also of increasing the divergence between the teachings of Sunday school and college. Squaring science and religion was, however, problematic until he studied the Bible more closely and found that the legends and myths that underscored the holy book's teachings contained profound truths. While he pondered over many big questions, he encountered two men at Morehouse who

Benjamin Elijah Mays (1895–1984), was the president of Morehouse College and a civil rights activist. Growing up in the rural South, he developed an 'insatiable desire' for education, all the more because of the segregated system. After attending Bates College in Lewiston, Maine and completing his PhD at the University of Chicago, he was an outstanding orator, whose broad social vision left a deep impression on King. They formed a close friendship that lasted for the rest of King's life and Mays delivered the eulogy at King's funeral.

provided much needed guidance: Dr Benjamin Mays, college president and Professor George Kelsey, who taught philosophy and religion. King admired both men for their religious faith, learning and confidence. He regarded them as worthy of emulation.

By the time of his senior year, his earlier religious doubts had disappeared and he entered the ministry. The call to serve as a minister was powerful and fully embraced. Now he could see clearly the influence of his father, the *great moving factor*, for whom his admiration had remained undimmed and whose example he was proud to follow.

When King departed from Morehouse, he was morally and ethically more mature. *My call to the ministry was not a miraculous or supernatural something*, he wrote. He was ready to give outward expression to the inner urge to serve humanity. And so, on 25 February 1948 he was ordained at Ebenezer Baptist Church.[18] A few months later, on 8 June, he received his Bachelor of Arts degree from Morehouse College.

King's studentship at Morehouse College taught him many things. He came to know that many poor whites were no less exploited that African-Americans and fundamentally that injustice was endemic in the American economic system.

He was not shy of expressing his feelings against capitalism in which his father believed. It was, therefore, inevitable that father and son would disagree. There were a few 'sharp exchanges'[19] and Daddy remembered raising his voice 'a few times'. Thus, the short, 'plump-faced youth, healthy, confident and questing' had little or no interest in accumulating wealth. Benjamin Mays recalled the young man's unusual seriousness and sensitivity.[20]

King's ideas about the economic system led him to target the Church. His father's presumption that his boys Martin and Alfred would also become preachers aroused unease in young Martin, who had been considering other careers such as law and medicine. While this was a form of rebellion against his father,[21] the real issue was King's reservations about the narrow thinking of the Baptist Church. Should not responsible black preachers query and challenge the caste system of the South based on race and colour? With few exceptions, historically, the black church seemed to have acquiesced in this oppressive system, while waiting for a dispensation from above. Complicity with the oppressor could/should not be condoned. The Church, the young King felt, had to more clearly think through its intellectually indefensible position.

In the period of questioning that followed, King was drawn into philosophical and theological discussions and through this he was able to dispel doubts about his desire to become a minister of the Church. So Morehouse, whose founders were white Baptists, had through the rigour of academic excellence, taught King the merits of combining 'moral integrity, intellectual enquiry and civic responsibility' that the College espoused.[22]

In a sense, Mays and Kelsey merely confirmed what King had already learned from his father. Daddy had taken a broad view of his pastoral role, regarding himself as a leader of Atlanta's black community. He was an organiser of voter registration drives, served as a board member of Morehouse College and was active in the National Association for the Advancement of Coloured People, the nation's leading Civil Rights organisation. While he did not espouse radical views, he could not separate religion from politics. He was careful that his son should know and appreciate the earlier struggles of African-

---

Booker T Washington (1856–1915) was an educator and race leader. Famous for the 'Atlanta Compromise', a speech in which he tried to impress both whites and blacks, Washington's 'accommodationist' strategy was an attempt to assuage white concerns by promising improved black economic productivity and assuring the elite that social integration was not a desired goal. After 1900, Washington came under increasing pressure from black opponents who questioned his approach to legalised segregation, loss of voting rights and violence against black people.

Americans which informed black history. He also showed his independence of mind by not joining popular denunciation of older leaders such as Booker T Washington.[23]

In the year that King became his father's assistant, desegregation in the US armed forces was ordered, black votes helped Harry Truman to election victory and Mahatma Gandhi was assassinated in India.

King was intent on counteracting the 'Negro stereotype', which he identified as always laughing, 'dirty and messy'. As a recently ordained preacher and with his sociology degree, King enrolled for a three-year course of study at Crozer Seminary in Chester, Pennsylvania.

At the age of 19, he was younger than his classmates and one of only 11 black students in the student body of 100. He arrived from a narrow, even fundamentalist tradition, but soon found that he could embrace the liberal interpretation of Christianity easily. He believed in man's *natural goodness* and the power of human reason.

At Crozer, King began his intellectual quest to find a way of eliminating social evil. He read some of the great philosophical texts by Plato, Aristotle, Rousseau, Thomas Hobbes, Jeremy Bentham, John Stuart Mill and Locke, benefiting greatly from his study of their social and ethical theories.

Then he came to Walter Rauschenbusch's *Christianity and the Social Crisis*, which provided him with a 'theological basis' for the social concerns that had arisen from his early experience. Rauschenbusch was a prominent social activist who tried to translate the lessons of the New Testament into a cohesive public policy programme. He argued, therefore, that the gospel not only offered personal salvation but had social implications, too.

After reading Rauschenbusch, King became more convinced of what religion and his role as a preacher should be. Religion, he argued, would be *spiritually moribund* if its concern for men's souls were not equated with the slums that damned them, the economic and social conditions that so debased and eventually destroyed them.[24]

Preaching, always in his blood, was the means of disseminating this message. As an aspirant to the ministry, King strove to be helpful, sincere and intelligent. He preferred being a preacher with 'spiritual power' rather than one who was just a spell-binder at the pulpit. A preacher, he reasoned, should get to know his congregation and the problems they faced. What's more, he needed to articulate his message in terms that his parishioners could understand. He saw preaching as a 'dual process' designed to change individuals and societies. Thus, his interest in employment, slums and economic insecurity was integral to his advocacy of the social gospel, which he did not compromise.

After Rauschenbusch, King moved on to the writings of Reinhold Niebuhr, a theologian and political journalist. Niebuhr's book *Moral Man and Immoral Society* argued that there was no moral difference when choosing between violent and non-violent resistance.[25] King praised Niebhur's work for helping him to *recognize the illusions of a superficial optimism concerning human nature and the dangers of a false idealism*, and given his belief in man's potential for good, he also attributed to Niebhur the guidance for his understanding of collective evil and the moral dilemmas that confronted Christians who were non-pacifists.

King's reading included Karl Marx's *Das Kapital* and the *Communist Manifesto*, and works on the thinking of Lenin. Among the conclusions he drew from these writings were a rejection of the materialist interpretation of history, his strong disagreement with communism's ethical relativism and his opposition to communism's political totalitarianism.

King regarded man as the *child of God* for whom the state was made and not the other way around. Central to this thought was the freedom of man, who should never be relegated to a *thing*, but should be elevated to the status of a person. He warned that man must never be devalued by the state to being the means to an end, but rather as *an end within himself*.

After reading Marx, King became convinced that truth was not to be found either in Marxism or in traditional capitalism. Given the particularity of each (he noted capitalism's failure to see the truth in collective enterprise and Marxism's failure to see the reality of individual enterprise) King stressed it was not a case of either or, but one of synthesis which reconciled the observations of both.

His study programme was intense, but not all-consuming; there was some latitude. Within weeks of arriving at Crozer, he confessed in a letter to his mother that he was popular with girls, all the more, he said, when the news spread that he was from a well-to-do family. Among those he dated was a white German girl. Their friendship was cause for concern among many people: a black-white relationship at that time was an explosive issue and when Pius Barbour, a family friend and former student at Crozer, heard of King's involvement, he had no doubt about his friend's next move. Another of King's friends, Ed Whitaker, agreed with Barbour's advice to King that the 'serious' love affair must be ended. Although this was easier said than done, for King did nothing half-heartedly, when, finally, he had ended the relationship, he was so 'broken-hearted' by the separation that according to Barbour, he 'never recovered'.[26]

Unsurprisingly, King excelled at Crozer. His confidence grew. He became president and valedictorian of his class, and being named 'most outstanding student' assured him of a scholarship for graduate study.

More important, the pragmatic King shifted with ease from academic theory to practice. Presciently, in a course paper entitled 'The Significant Contributions of Jeremiah to Religious Thought', he wrote about the American establishment, the

Mohandas Karamchand Gandhi (1869–1948), the 'Mahatma', was the pre-eminent figure of India's independence movement. After training as a lawyer in England, he moved to South Africa and soon made his mark as a campaigner for Indian rights. It was here that he conceived his philosophy of non-violent resistance or satyagraha, which advocated refusing to cooperate with anything perceived as wrong without resorting to violence. He returned to India in 1914 and within a few years was leading a nationwide movement for home rule. A year after independence, Gandhi was assassinated by a Hindu fanatic.

sponsors of which detracted from Christianity, and warned against religion giving its blessings to the status quo.

At about the same time, King travelled to Philadelphia to attend a sermon delivered by Dr Mordecai Johnson, President of Howard University, who had just returned from India. Dr Johnson's theme was the life and teachings of Mahatma Gandhi.

Gandhi's *satyagraha*, the campaign of non-violent resistance which he led against British rule in India, struck a deep chord in King. He was smitten by the inner strength and power of the frail-looking Indian and nothing was so profound in helping to open up King's fertile mind as he studied the mechanics of social change. He would later write that Gandhi was *probably the first person in history to lift the love ethic of Jesus above mere interaction between individuals to a powerful and effective social force*. In Gandhi's philosophy he found an intellectual and moral satisfaction that was lacking in the utilitarianism of Bentham and Mill, Marx and Lenin, Hobbes, Rousseau and Nietzsche.

Up to this point, King's intellectual journey had led him to discover a means through which Christians could deal with personal and social evils, including the evils of race prejudice and economic injustice. What is more, he was able to assess capitalism and communism as falling far short of delivering social justice. Gandhi, however, was the embodiment of the thoughts and ideas that he had been considering. Through Gandhi, he was able to think through the problem of making the 'love ethic' of Jesus an integral part of resisting evil, and by facing it head-on help to bring about meaningful change in society. There was nothing passive about the resistance that he was contemplating. It was non-violent resistance to evil that struck him as being a social force on a large scale.[27]

Boston University

In May 1951, King left Crozer with a Bachelor of Divinity degree. But he still yearned for more intensive study. He targeted Boston University as the place where he would do his postgraduate work, particularly because it would give him the opportunity of benefiting from the tutelage of scholars such as Dr Edgar Brightman (whose book *A Philosophy of Religion*, King had already read) and L Harold De Wolf.

But while he followed his intellectual journey, King had to confront the problem of racial bias in housing. As he put it, the rooms he had hoped to live in were for rent until the landlord realised he was an African-American. Then, suddenly, the room had *just been rented*. This rebuff must have caused unease, though he seemed to take it in his stride.

Meanwhile, he proceeded to learn all he could at the university's School of Theology, the oldest Methodist seminary in the US. Here, he was in contact with many exponents of pacifism, non-violence and the social gospel, including Howard Thurman, Dean of the University Chapel, an African-American preacher and writer. Thurman had known Daddy King at Morehouse and by the time of King's final year at Boston University, he and Thurman had become good friends.[28]

He also received instruction from De Wolf and Peter Bertocci, a colleague of De Wolf's at Boston University, on 'Personalism' which held the view that the 'human personality comprising all individual persons constituted the 'ultimate intrinsic value in the world'. From this, King deduced that if the dignity and worth of all human personalities was the ultimate value in the world, racial segregation and discrimination were among the world's ultimate evils.[29] This helped him to realise the value of religion as a personal experience of God that was both human and divine. Through this experience, he had hoped to find the meaning of *ultimate reality*.

As King delved more deeply into modern philosophy and theology, he tried to reconcile Niebuhr's critique of liberalism with his own optimistic view of human nature, his abhorrence of war and the need for social justice. Above all, he developed a concept of God that confirmed his optimism about human personality.

Throughout his time in Boston, King frequently developed a reputation as a powerful orator. He returned to Atlanta whenever possible, keeping strong the ties to his family and to the church there.

The Boston years present an image of the youthful King as unrebellious and rather conventional. He was a model son, student and easy-going companion who felt at home in school or college. He liked good suits and had expensive tastes which he was able to afford.[30]

Coretta, Courtship and Marriage

Among his fellow-students, the bright, personable King shone. He was not shy, he dressed well and unsurprisingly he was attractive to the opposite sex. He was a party-goer who enjoyed life, but he was dissatisfied with the young women around him. They were, he confided in his friend Mary Powell, disappointing compared with those from the South. Ms Powell suggested the name of one of her fellow-students, Coretta Scott, who was from Alabama. King took a chance. Soon, he was on the phone to Ms Scott to ask for a date. They agreed to meet.

Coretta Scott was born in Marion, Alabama and had attended

Antioch College in Ohio. Having inherited a talent for music from her mother, she was determined to develop it. Her ambition was to be a concert singer and with the help of a scholarship, she attended the New England Conservatory in Boston, where she worked diligently to develop her mezzo-soprano voice.[31]

During his courtship, Martin went to all lengths. He was full of compliments and Coretta received them graciously. In a relatively short time, she was able to form an opinion of him. A good talker, King behaved like 'a typical man', the proud possessor of 'smoothness' and 'jive,' which Coretta said, she 'kind of enjoyed'. Small and short, King was soon able to make up for his unimpressive physical size; he was so charming that Coretta quickly conceded being impressed. In the first months of 1952, they saw a good deal of each other and, at times, she accompanied him when he attended discussions on philosophy, politics and race. Through this period and in later years, she was struck by his playfulness and humour even in the gravest situations.[32]

It was at this time, she said, that Martin first expressed his interest in 'the masses' and the skewed distribution of wealth in America. She listened attentively, enthralled. The ownership of so much by so few people troubled Martin who was against capitalism and regarded his father, a capitalist, as a man who 'loved money', importantly only for his family, but significantly not for 'the rest of humanity'.

As always, the student King kept in close touch with his home and family in Atlanta, returning there in the summer of 1952 to help Daddy. On his visits home, King, Jr, did pulpit work, preaching the gospel. On one such visit he saw one of his former girlfriends and admitted this to Coretta. But by August, his courtship of Coretta had reached a critical stage. They decided that Coretta should visit his parents.

She must have wondered how she would be received. Martin had many women friends in Atlanta and predictably his father had hoped he would marry one of them. Though Mary Powell may have informed Coretta of Martin's Atlanta past, Coretta kept an open mind. She remained close, supportive and was among the congregation in Ebenezer Church to hear Martin give an impressive preaching performance. If his passion was unforgettable, so too were his parents' cool attitude towards Coretta.

On their return to Boston, Martin and Coretta's courtship continued.[33] A few months later, Martin's parents visited him in a last-ditch attempt to persuade him and his loved one to end their romance. The no-nonsense father felt it was his responsibility to secure his son's future by pressing him to complete his education and return to Atlanta where young women from respected families awaited his marriage proposal. When this stark message was put to Coretta, she replied that she too came from a family no less respected. Martin's silence during this exchange was, it seemed, powerful enough to convince his father of his future with Coretta. The strength of feeling, the bonding between the lovers saw them through subsequent difficulties and early in the following year, 1953, they were engaged.[34]

In June, Daddy King presided at the wedding ceremony held in the garden of Coretta's family home in Perry County, Alabama.[35] Alfred Daniel, Martin's brother, was best man and, for better or worse, the married couple's first night was spent in the house of an undertaker, who was a close friend of the Scott family. A couple of days later, they travelled back to the King home in Atlanta.

By the autumn, they had returned to Boston where King resumed his studies. He was now on the brink of his doctoral programme and senior staff were on hand to advise him. Many, including De Wolf and other instructors, whom he trusted, were keen that he should have a career in the university as a teacher. But this was not the stuff of which Martin Luther King, Jr was made. Unswerving from his path, he decided to become a Minister of the Church, an outcome which should have surprised no one.

On 25 January 1954, the day that King arrived in Montgomery from Boston to give his trial sermon at the Dexter Avenue Baptist Church, he was anxious, conscious that he was on trial. At 11am, he was at the pulpit, poised to deliver his sermon entitled: 'The Three Dimensions of a Complete Life'. This would become one of the most famous of his sermons. In part, this is what he said:

The length of life, as we shall use it, is not its duration not its longevity. It is rather the push of a life forward to its personal welfare. The breadth of a life is the outward concern for the welfare of others. The height of a life is the upward reach toward God. These are the three dimensions of life and, without the due development of all, no life becomes complete. Life at its best is a great triangle. At one angle stands the individual person, at the other angle stands other persons, and at the top stands God. Unless these three are concatenated, working harmoniously together in a single life, that life is incomplete.

The congregation was receptive but the pulpit committee needed time to deliberate. A month later, King received a letter from Montgomery with the news that the committee was unanimous in offering him the pastorate of the Dexter Avenue Baptist Church. Though he was *very happy* he delayed his reply because he was, even at this late stage, *torn in two directions*: should he follow work as a pastor or should he devote his time to education?

He discussed the matter with Coretta and finally they agreed that their 'greatest service' was to make a contribution to their native Southland. They felt morally obliged to do so, for a few years at least. And given the problem of racial discrimination, they wanted to be active in the movement for change which they sensed in the South.

Although he needed more time to complete his doctoral thesis, King undertook his pastoral duties full-time from 1 September 1954, and had earlier, one Sunday in May 1954, he preached his first sermon as a minister of the Dexter Avenue Baptist Church, marking the end of a stretch of 21 years of uninterrupted schooling. Nonetheless, the 'residential requirements' for his PhD degree had to be completed. He worked diligently at the task of writing his thesis. Before its completion, however (as if reviewing his life thus far and also justifying his religious commitment) he was very much engaged in the process of 'rediscovering lost values.' He was preoccupied with the thought that the world needed men and women who were strong enough to uphold what was right and oppose what was wrong for, *If we are to go forward we must go back and rediscover...that all reality has spiritual control.*[36]

From the pulpit, he was modest and humble. He told the congregation that he had *nothing special* to offer and regarded himself neither as a *great preacher* nor as a *profound scholar*. But, he said, it was his calling not only to preach, but also to lead God's people.[37]

Almost two months after he had been at the parsonage as a full-time pastor, his formal installation as Dexter's minister was graced with the presence of Daddy who delivered the Sermon. Here, in his proud father's presence, the son had come to terms with the call.[38]

Throughout his years at Seminary, King remained grounded in the history and culture of the black Church.[39] There was no shortage of passion and emotional power among Baptist preachers, whose sermons were accompanied by the uninhibited participation of their congregations in the form of shouts, clapping, feet-stamping, laughter and tears. Long recitations of Biblical passages were accompanied by a music hall atmosphere, as choir-led congregations sang spirituals and hymns like nobody else.

They sang about their troubles and freedom in *There is a Balm in Gilead, Go Down Moses* and *Hold On* which addressed African-Americans' bondage in verses such as: 'The only time we did right/Was the day we began our fight/Keep your eyes on the prize/Hold on.'[40]

From the outset, time had to be carefully managed. Each day, King rose early and spent three hours writing his thesis. He spent the rest of the day on Church work which did not include the weekly service, marriages, funerals and personal conferences, visiting and praying with the sick and maimed.

King immersed himself in Montgomery's social and economic problems, so much so that he insisted on members of his Church registering to vote and joining the NAACP. To raise social and political awareness and involvement, King also formed a social and political action committee, which included Jo Ann Robinson, a white woman, and Rufus Lewis as its members. King himself was an active member of the local branch, especially on matters as they related to the Courts.

King also became interested in the Alabama Christian Movement for Human Rights, a rare interracial organisation which worked through educational methods for equal opportunities for both white and black people in Alabama. King was elected vice-president of the body which had a small membership but played a central role. It was the only interracial group in Montgomery and, in spite of the obvious dangers, King felt its existence was vital because it helped to maintain a much needed dialogue between the segregated racial groups.

As it was, King's liberal views were too much even for his own

> The National Association for the Advancement of Colored People (NAACP) is the oldest and largest civil rights organisation in the US. Founded by a multiracial group of activists, including W E B DuBois, it was set up to secure political, educational, social and economic equality for African-Americans through litigation, political activity and public education. Its successful campaigns include the Supreme Court ruling in 1954 that segregation in state schools was unconstitutional.

black people who were, among other reasons, unable to reconcile his interest in both the NAACP and the ACMHR. While many African-Americans felt that legislation and Court action were the only means of effecting integration, for some white people, integration was possible only through education. King's dialectical reasoning was, therefore, not well-received. The worry for his opponents was that he was giving allegiance to organisations that were in direct opposition. He responded by opposing a one-dimensional approach to the *race problem*. Education was the key, for through it attitudes and feelings (prejudice and hate) could be changed. Legislation and the Courts, he argued were, of course, there to *regulate behaviour*. Thus, instead of the singular approach, two or more strategies were preferable

At about this time, from the pulpit at Dexter, King spoke out saying that to generalize about all white people being the same is a temptation that must be resisted. The acts of one or a few whites who were negative did not implicate all white people. This statement came from the heart, from his own experience and masterfully he related it to the fact that the much-respected NAACP was instituted by whites and had the support of white people from both the north and the South.[41]

More than a year after his arrival at Dexter Avenue Baptist Church, the Kings first child Yolanda Denise was born.[42] She kept her father 'busy,' as he learned more and more about fatherhood and his demanding ministry.

Earlier, in one of his Sermons, he had spoken about his service to this historic church saying how *dreadfully aware* he was of his heavy responsibilities which he described as staggering and astounding. It was during this period while he was also busy with Yoki that he received news that would bring even greater responsibilities than he already had, responsibilities that would push him forward and tax him as never before.

What King sought through his sermonic pronouncements

were love and justice and freedom in the here and now. From the hugely disappointing old South, he was intent upon ushering a new world. So, it was against this background of religion and learning that the young King reached out to the people of his newly adopted Montgomery community.

Montgomery's moment of truth

Like all other Southern cities, Montgomery's buses were segregated.[43] On the first day of December 1955, Rosa Parks, a seamstress and local NAACP activist, refused to vacate her seat on a city bus. Her arrest, sparked a revolt that had long been simmering among African-Americans in the city. Clearly, Mrs Parks had had enough and her action was respected by the majority of African-Americans in Montgomery.

At this time, a confluence of factors had become potentially explosive. Mrs Parks, a seasoned campaigner for social change in the South was fully aware of the consequences of her radical

King addressing a civil rights campaign meeting, Rosa Parks is seated in the front row

action, knowing well of an earlier challenge by the Women's Political Council for change in the segregated bus system.[44] She was highly regarded by many in the black community and according to King, she became a victim of the *forces of history and the forces of destiny*. She was the trigger blessed with a character that was impeccable and with deep-rooted dedication.

Early on the morning of the day after the arrest of Mrs Parks, E D Nixon, another activist, who had signed the bond to release Parks, telephoned King to relate the incident. King was deeply shocked and Nixon ended his call by saying that a boycott of the buses was the only way forward. Anything less than this would not get the message across to prejudiced white people. He argued that African-Americans would no longer submit to unfair treatment. King agreed with Nixon as did a young minister of Montgomery's First Baptist Church, the Rev. Ralph Abernathy.

Ralph Abernathy (1926-90) the minister and civil rights leader, was an early ally of King's. While Abernathy focused on tactics, King was concerned with how best to put the strategy into action. Abernathy is best described as King's pastor, giving him counsel, solace and perspective. Abernathy's autobiography *And the Walls Come Tumbling Down* was widely acclaimed as a study of the inner workings of the civil rights movement but it also, generated controversy because it acknowledged King's extra-marital affairs.

The next move, Nixon and King agreed, was to convene a public meeting of Montgomery's religious and political leaders to discuss the idea and implementation of a proposal to boycott the buses. King suggested that they meet that same evening in his Church. Just before the meeting, King said he was filled with joy, for he knew that at last *something unusual was about to happen*. A Committee was formed and a statement was released requesting African-Americans not to ride the bus to work, to town, to school, or any place on Monday 5 December. All were invited to attend a mass meeting that Monday at 7pm at the Holt Street Baptist Church for *further instruction*.

The Committee also agreed to form the Montgomery Improvement Association and King was elected President. His excitement was such that it affected his sleep pattern. The next day, with the help of an *army* of local people, thousands of leaflets were distributed in the city.

At this time, bus segregation was one of the most sensitive aspects of life in Montgomery. It was an intolerable situation for African-Americans to whom insult was added to injury when bus operators and conductors referred to them as 'niggers' and 'black apes.' Each day black passengers were reminded that they could not sit on the first four empty seats reserved for white passengers.[45] Transgression of this arrangement meant immediate arrest, charges and imprisonment.

Against this background and after reading about the proposed boycott, King's reasoning powers came to the fore. He began to have reservations about the 'nature' of the action to be taken. How should it be carried out? He was unsure of justifying the means with the ends of the boycott. For him morality had to be the very basis of what the Committee had to achieve. Weighing up the pros and cons, he concluded that justice and freedom should be the goals of the boycott method and he was careful to stress the importance of introducing justice into business, not bankruptcy to the bus company. Why? Because he linked local business with an 'evil system' and felt that instead of using the word boycott (which, with time, he used less frequently) he regarded the Montgomery bus protest as an *act of massive non-co-operation*.

To King's surprise, during the morning rush hour on 5 December, the first day of the boycott, the African-American community's response was almost total. He was astonished and declared that a miracle had taken place. Later that morning a crowd had gathered at the courthouse where Mrs Parks was to be tried. She was found guilty and fined ten dollars. She appealed.

After an unusually busy day, King had less than half-an-hour to make what was hitherto the 'most decisive' speech of his life. He had only time to sketch out what he was going to say to perhaps the largest audience he had ever addressed. And this was all the more testing because he was a relative newcomer to Montgomery. He was just 26 years old.

On the night of the mass meeting, the church was tightly packed as King made his way to the pulpit. As the echo of the hymn 'Onward Christian Soldiers' faded the large audience became remarkably quiet, expectant. King stood facing the congregation. His resonant voice filled the church as he reviewed the difficulties imposed by an unjust system upon the African-American people who rode on Montgomery's buses. *We are here this evening for serious business*, he said. *We are here in a general sense because first and foremost we are American citizens and we are determined to apply our citizenship to the fullness of its meaning...* He talked about his people's disinheritance and their tiredness of having endured the *long night of captivity*. Now, of necessity, their quest was for freedom, justice, equality, not the tools of persuasion and coercion. Why? Because such goals were only achievable through education and legislation.

He recognised the importance of that historic moment and asked each one to be courageous and determined in working together. In his rallying call, he concluded with pride and an immediacy rare among American religious leaders, by saying that history could not ignore a race of people with 'fleecy locks and black complexion,' who stood up for rights, a people who added 'new meaning' to history and civilization.

When King sat down the people rose to their feet. The applause took a while to die down. Then he read the words of his Committee's three-point resolution which he put to the meeting, calling upon African-Americans to stay off the buses until first, courteous treatment by the bus operators was guaranteed; second, passengers were seated on a first come, first served basis – 'Negroes' seating from the back of the bus toward the front, whites from the front toward the back; and third, black bus operators should be employed on predominantly 'Negro routes'.[45] This was carried unanimously to resounding cheers.

But even though he had become fully engaged by the time that 'day of days' 5 December 1955 had ended, King remembered it well: On his way home that night, he was heartened. He felt privileged to have been part of the experience and to have borne witness to something truly amazing. The thousands who had attended the mass meeting standing together with self-discipline and unity of purpose, with a new sense of dignity and destiny. Thus began a national movement that astounded defenders of the status quo and infused new hope among African-Americans. That night of 5 December, King said was Montgomery's *moment of history*.

Less than two weeks later on 17 December the first major effect of the mass meeting was that King and other MIA leaders met with white representatives. Although this attempt to resolve the bus dispute was unsuccessful, it was a step in the right direction.

From the outset of the boycott, the Movement was guided by Christian love. King became increasingly aware of Mahatma Gandhi's inspiration. He realised early that love, as advocated in Christianity and if channelled through Gandhian non-violence was a major option in the African-Americans' struggle for freedom.

Coincidentally, just a few days into the protest, Ms Juliette Morgan, a white woman, who understood and sympathised with the Movement, wrote to the *Montgomery Advertiser*. Bravely, she compared the Gandhian movement in India with the local protest. At the time, this was a radical thing to have done. Thereafter, Ms Morgan was criticised and rejected by many people in the white community.

But already the matter had become integral to larger issues. Morgan's letter heartened King who advanced non-violent resistance as the movement's guiding force, and love as the *regulating ideal*. Put simply, Christ provided the 'spirit and motivation,' while Gandhi furnished the method.[46]

As this new philosophy became more evident, the people of Montgomery responded to non-violence in a variety of ways. While it was true to say that the process was gradual, members of the executive board were privately concerned that a more radical approach was not taken. They saw non-violence as ineffective while others felt some violence was necessary to impress upon white people the seriousness of African-Americans. Nonetheless, most of them were enamoured of the Gandhian technique and regarded it as a positive step forward.

In his mid-20s, everything that King had learned so far had, it seemed, prepared him for this leadership. But as the bus boycott persisted, for King, the days to come would be testing.[47]

The city of Montgomery officials did not expect the first days of success of the bus boycott to last. Even the rain which they had hoped would dampen the spirit of the protesters and force them back on to the empty buses had failed to do so.

Eventually, when both sides came together to negotiate a settlement, it became clear to King, *a victim of unwarranted optimism* that the illusion of the privileged surrendering their position of advantage on request was unrealistic. Privileges were hard-won.

After the first round of negotiations, the MIA executive agreed not to budge from their three proposals. King and the organisers braced themselves for the likelihood of a long struggle. For one thing, they would have to provide alternative transport facilities for Montgomery's 50,000 non-white people. They would also need to rethink their strategy: for example, should they go beyond their initial proposals and demand the abolition of bus segregation?[47]

Increasingly, as King faced many new and trying moments, his refuge was home and closeness to Coretta, whose calm and soothing voice whenever she sang, gave him renewed strength. She was the rock upon which his marriage and civil rights leadership, especially at this time of crisis, was founded.

Attempts by city officials to divide and weaken the protestors persisted and for the first time, King began to question the commitment of his people to press on with the struggle. Such doubts prompted him to lead by example and let himself be subsumed by the protest. But in so doing, he felt obliged to declare his dispensability at a mass meeting: *I want you to know that if Martin Luther King had never been born this movement would have taken place. I just happened to be here. You know there comes a time when time itself is ready for change. That time has come for Montgomery, and I had nothing to do with it.*[48]

King's statement was well-timed. Under the 'get tough' policy of the authorities, he was arrested and jailed for driving in excess of the speed limit – according to the policeman who had trailed him, he was allegedly doing 30 miles an hour in a 25-mile-an-hour zone.

It was King's first spell of imprisonment and he was joined by his good friend Ralph Abernathy. When a large crowd gathered outside, both were released but King admitted that his night in prison had merely strengthened his commitment to the struggle.

Another consequence of the escalating protest was the threats King received in telephone calls and letters that had, by January 1956, increased to 40 a day. While the threat was real, he was careful to retain his dignity and discipline. At one mass meeting, he spoke again of the non-violent protest being maintained whether he was dead or alive. But already his leadership was being seen as special.

With the movement still in its infancy, Glen Smiley wrote a letter which he copied to a number of people in the Fellowship of Reconciliation, an inter-faith organisation: 'The die has been cast, there is a crisis of terrifying intensity, and I believe that God has called Martin Luther King, Jr. to lead a great movement here in the South. But why does God lay such a burden on one so young, so inexperienced, so good? King can be a Negro Gandhi... That is why I am writing [to] more than two dozen people of prayer across the nation, asking that they hold Martin Luther King in the light. Of his own free will, he has sought counsel from some of us older. May he burst like fruit out of season, into the type of leader required for this hour.'[49]

King needed all the inner strength and external support he could muster. But at this time, he was beset by self-doubt. He had plunged to new depths of despair when late one night he picked up his phone to hear a caller say: 'Listen nigger, we've taken all we want from you; before next week you'll be sorry you ever came to Montgomery.' The call deeply disturbed King. He could not get back to sleep. He paced about the kitchen. He was tempted to call Daddy as he had always done when he needed him. Instead, he got on his knees and prayed for confirmation that what he was doing was right. He prayed for strength and courage to lead his followers and to address their urgent needs. He spoke with increasing desperation: *I am at the end of my powers. I have nothing left. I've come to the point where I can't face it alone.* After these words, an *inner voice* called upon him to stand up for righteousness, justice and truth even *until the end of the world.*

King added that he had heard the voice of Jesus urging him on and promised to be at his side. At that moment, he felt he was in the presence of the Divine and soon his fears, his insecurity disappeared and he was prepared to carry the fight forward, to *face anything.*[50]

So by the end of that darkest of nights, the moment of crisis had passed; and once more, he braced himself for the unenviable task ahead.

*

Three nights later, while he was attending a mass meeting, a bomb exploded in the porch of the King's residence. Coretta and Yoki were in the rear section of the house at the time. When news reached the mass meeting, King was the last to be informed. For quite a while, until he reached the house, he did not know if his wife and child were hurt. When, at last, he saw them, he was relieved and overjoyed to see them unharmed.

By this time, a large crowd had gathered outside King's home. In the highly charged atmosphere, the white mayor and police commissioner who were present looked 'very pale'. Amid this awkward, surreal situation, from his damaged porch, King addressed his people: he requested that no weapons be used; non-violence and love were the goals. *Love your enemies*, he said, *Be good to them*. For many, it was a bitter pill to swallow. King reiterated his role in the boycott, saying he did not start it, but if he was stopped, the movement and its work would certainly continue. The righteousness of the protest was not in question for he believed God was on the side of the campaigners.[51]

After he spoke, shouts of 'Amen' and 'God bless you' issued from the crowd. Many people were in tears. And for the first time, King referred to the country as a whole, letting it be known that from Montgomery he was addressing all Americans. The bus protest was not a parochial matter; it had national resonance.

If the American public was none the wiser about the meaning of the boycott, King was intent on making it clearer. In the *New York Times*, he wrote that the African-American-led action in Montgomery was not a hate campaign. It was certainly not a war between black and white Americans, but a stand against crass injustice and a struggle for human rights. He advocated love, compassion, understanding and he wrote of his fellow-boycotters being on the *threshold of a new dawn*.[52]

His hope for such a dawn was, however, quickly shattered. As if to stoke the fires of hate, some 48 hours after the explosion on

King's porch, dynamite was thrown on to E D Nixon's lawn. Miraculously, there were no casualties. Nonetheless, in the aftermath of these attempts to maim and kill leaders of the protest movement, King's friends were convinced that he needed to be protected by bodyguards and that armed men should guard his house. Daddy King agreed. But King insisted he was unafraid and, therefore, did not need a weapon to protect himself. For him, it was the weapon of love that should be aimed for, not the use of a gun. When, under pressure from friends, he eventually applied for a weapon, his application was denied by the Sheriff's office. This was fortuitous for it gave King the chance to re-assess his position vis-à-vis carrying firearms: *How could I serve as one of the leaders of a non-violent movement and at the same time use weapons of violence for my personal protection?*

Once more, he turned to Coretta for counsel. If those around him were fearful, he seemed at peace with himself. *Had we become distracted by the question of my safety,* he wrote later, *we would have lost the moral offensive and sunk to the level of our oppressors.*[53]

Tactically, the protest had nullified the violence from the opposing forces. But it took a new turn as mass arrests were ordered when an old law was invoked to make the boycott illegal. King and Abernathy were among those indicted. The effect on the morale of the protesters was King's principal worry for he knew how hard pressed they had been over 13 weeks.

When he was indicted, King was lecturing at Fisk University in Nashville, Tennessee. On his return to Atlanta he was met at the airport by Coretta, his mother and father, they were afraid, depressed and worried. The strain of being Martin Luther King, Jr, had implications for everyone around him. His father urged him not to return to Montgomery, impressing upon his son that of all those who were indicted, the authorities primary goal was 'to get you'.

Be that as it may, the shift in King's thinking from his own

King photographed in the Police Station Birmingham Alabama

safety to being true to himself, kept him focused. His course was set, his destiny mapped out. Anything less than a total commitment to the movement would be tantamount to a lack of moral courage to commit himself to the struggle, whatever the consequences.[54] Eventually, even Daddy understood his son's destiny.

Instead of feeling tarred by the judgement of an all-white jury, King said he was proud of his *crime*. He described the crowd scene at the jail as jolly, as having something of a *holiday atmosphere*. People, it seemed, were eager to get arrested. Fear was not evident, but his pride in being held for resisting oppression shone through.

King felt the sense of solidarity shored him up as he walked steadfastly towards the jail and soon after the bond for his release was paid he made his way home. Finally, on the day of his trial, he was brought before Judge Eugene Carter and a guilty verdict was delivered for 'violating the state's anti-boycott law'. His penalty included a $500 fine, court costs, or 386 days of hard labour. The Judge felt that King warranted the minimum penalty, a lenient sentence which he argued was justified because of King's determination to avoid violence. Outside the court, media interest had heightened. When King emerged from the building, he faced several television cameras and photographers. Mindful of the importance of their role, he waved to his supporters as he was driven away.

For King, the verdict was a judgment against all African-Americans. But ultimately, he believed that each person must stand up for his or her beliefs. Gradually, he was enlarging his vision. He saw his triumph over the paralysis of *crippling fear* as a motivating factor in uplifting not only African-Americans but humanity as a whole. He praised his church supporters and Coretta, the rock beside him, the wife who never failed to give him hope.[55]

He hoped for a *glorious daybreak*, but the movement's difficulties loomed ever larger. The city's decision to bring legal action against the movement's car pool, which was used to transport people to and from work and on other essential journeys, led to another scheduled court hearing. King was at the forefront of the pool's activities and on the morning of the hearing, during a recess at about noon, he was aware of *unusual commotion* in the courtroom. Montgomery Commissioners and Mayor Gayle were summoned to a back-room, which reporters entered and left. King looked to his attorneys for an explanation. Moments later, a reporter handed King a piece of paper and said it was the decision that 'you have been waiting for.' What King read were historic words conveying the message of the Supreme Court's decision that Alabama's State and local laws requiring segregation on buses were unconstitutional.[56]

At that moment, King felt an *inexpressible* joy. After informing the attorneys beside him, he rushed to the back of the courtroom and broke the joyous news to Coretta, Abernathy and E D Nixon. Then, like a ripple, word spread through the Court.

Amid the euphoria, King led a mass meeting the following night at which he said the people must decide the next move: should the protest be called off? He and his fellow MIA leaders anticipated a large attendance and instead of one, two meetings were held at opposite locations in town. The speakers – including King – shuttled between meetings, each of which unanimously agreed to end the protest, but not to return to the buses until the ruling came into effect.

As King and the MIA knew well, nothing could be taken for granted. At another mass meeting held on 20 December 1956, they were careful to provide everyone, especially black Montgomerians, with guidelines before they returned as passengers on the buses. King spoke about the protesters' 12-month ordeal and urged them to exercise restraint for if violence was used, they would have walked in vain for a year. Their return to the buses, he said, must be with the intention of turning enemies into friends through the transforming power of love. The crucial shift now was from protest to reconciliation. King harked back to the presence of God which he felt in Montgomery and hoped that goodwill between African-Americans and white Americans would prevail. Then he used perhaps his favourite metaphors at this time – darkness and light: *With this dedication (to reconciliation) we will be able to emerge from the bleak and desolate midnight of man's inhumanity to man to the bright and glittering daybreak of freedom and justice.*

The echo of his voice was quickly overlaid with loud, prolonged applause. The victory for King and his fellow-campaigners had come none too soon. Now it had to be savoured and, of course, tested.

The next morning was Montgomery's moment of truth, its 'new beginning.' Having been in the thick of things, King thought it was his duty to be present. He was up early and accompanied by Abernathy, Nixon, Glen Smiley, photographers and pressmen, he led the way to the bus stop. When the first bus came and the door opened, King stepped on and was greeted by a smiling driver who recognised him.

'I believe you are Reverend King, aren't you?'

Yes, King answered. *I am.*

'We are glad to have you this morning', the white driver said.

King thanked him and sat down. Those with him followed his example. Smiley, a white man, sat next to King. Their togetherness was powerfully symbolic. King smiled. By the end of that historic day, the *Montgomery Advertiser* reported that this significant change in the city's way of life had arrived in relative peace.[57]

The Montgomery bus movement was the first sustained mass protest in the South, and the first case of non-violent revolt in the country. Its effect upon the people of Montgomery was profound. The collective response to white oppression was the argument of black people in a struggle to *secure moral ends through moral means*. This was a creative force, wholly new to the American social battleground. Through this process, the nameless were beginning to feel empowered. They had not only acquired a sense of self respect, but also a strong determination to confront the barriers to freedom. There was no going back.

Now King had to convince oppressed African-Americans elsewhere, especially in the South, of their seminal contribution to freeing themselves from injustice through non-violent means and, thus, advance the process of reinvigorating American democracy. Reflecting on the experience of the boycott, King said it had taught him more about non-violence than any of the books he had read. So far, thoughtfulness and experience had taught him to appreciate the real value of non-violent political action.[58] But as the struggle for justice and freedom now spread among African-Americans, it provoked a white backlash.

Beyond Montgomery

Flush with the success of Montgomery, King was acutely conscious of his and the movement's role in local, national and world affairs. In his words: *History has thrust upon our generation an indescribably important destiny – to complete a process of democratisation which our nation has too long developed too slowly, but which is our most powerful weapon for world respect and emulation. How we deal with this crucial situation will determine our moral health as individuals, our cultural health as a region, our political health as a nation and our prestige as a leader of the free world.*[59]

In early 1957, King was awakened by a telephone call from Ralph Abernathy's wife Juanita saying that their home had been bombed. In another call, he was told that Abernathy's First Baptist Church was also hit. In these desperate, depressing moments, King knew *no words* to comfort his friend. There would be three more explosions in the city.

The men prayed together asking God for the strength and courage to remain steadfast in the path they had chosen. They toured the bombed sites and that afternoon, King travelled to meet other black civil rights leaders in Atlanta. He met people who were uplifted by the Montgomery experience and ready to bring into being a 'Southern movement' that would ensure implementation of the law against bus segregation. Unsurprisingly, he was voted president of the newly-formed Southern Christian Leadership Conference (SCLC). The pressure on him was enormous, as he preached, lectured, gave speeches, wrote letters and raised funds. Soon, he came to personify the anti-segregation challenge.[60]

He was articulate, courageous and a man of integrity. But he also possessed a balanced temperament which underscored impressive displays at the pulpit. In the constant danger and chaotic scenes that surrounded him, his self-control inspired calmness which made him the ideal person to mediate the fractious nature of the civil rights movement.[61]

On his return to Montgomery, King found that bombings had again taken its toll on the black community and the buses had been withdrawn as a result of the violent acts of white racists. He admitted to feeling discouraged and guilty for he felt responsible for all that was taking place in the city.

Events in Montgomery made headline news far and wide, featuring as *Time* magazine's cover story in February 1957. Now the genie of Montgomery was out of the bottle, and King remarked that there was less tension and less negativity towards him and the movement.[62]

Meanwhile, as his reputation and fame continued to spread throughout America, he was easily recognised wherever he went as the Rev King of Alabama. He had become *something special*. His awareness of being a *symbol* led him to wonder if he was worthy of the high principles and trust attributed to him by the people.

King on the cover of *Time* Magazine

Fame had, indeed, brought fear, bewilderment, frustration and exhaustion. Months into the

Montgomery protest, he admitted that he hardly had time to breathe.' His cool façade was tested. He felt disoriented by being so well-known, and admitted that he was finding it difficult to study and think.

Nonetheless, he pressed on with his work. Observers, many of them his critics, wondered what drove him: Ella Baker, one of the movement's staff members, thought he was seeking fame; and Stanley Levison, who was also closely associated with King, believed that the attention focused upon King helped to strengthen his resolve.[63]

In March 1957, King's high profile earned him an invitation to attend the celebrations of Ghana becoming the first African colony to achieve independence. The former British colony known as the Gold Coast was about to be reborn under the charismatic leadership of Kwame Nkrumah.

Nkrumah delivered a passionate speech of inspiration. 'We are no longer a British colony,' he said. 'We are a free and sovereign people.' Then the old flag came down and a new flag was hoisted to the uplifting shouts of 'Freedom! Freedom! Freedom!' King cried for joy and he could hear the words of a well-known Negro Spiritual, which he often quoted in his speeches, crying out: 'Free at last, free at last, Great God Almighty, I'm free at last.'[64]

For African-Americans who felt 'colonized' in America, the independence of Ghana sent out a powerful message. It symbolised hope for millions of oppressed peoples all over the world, and it strengthened King's belief in the triumph of justice. Of this historic moment of Black Power, he later wrote: *So the day finally came. About midnight on a dark night in 1957 a new nation came into being. That was a great hour... People came from all over the world – seventy nations... It was a beautiful experience to see some of the leading persons on the scene of the civil rights movement in America on hand.*

Martin Luther and Coretta King attend Ghana's independence ceremonies

And when he returned to America at the end of March, he was forever reminded of Prime Minister Nkrumah's powerful statement: 'I prefer self-government with danger to servitude with tranquillity.'[65]

Fresh from his travels, in April 1957 King spoke once more about dealing with his fame. From the mountain top, where could he go next? Hitting the heights so young – he was only 28 years old – his life could become something of a *decrescendo*. He confessed to being worried about peaking so soon, and there were huge expectations placed on him. But he was far too conscientious and realistic to become ensnared in unrealistic expectations.[66]

More and more, he sought solace and guidance in prayers. He reminded himself that he had been placed in this position with the help of others and recognised his roles both as a servant and maker of history. From his vantage point, he recognised that while progress had been made in Montgomery since 5 December 1955, the city's racial problems were no less intractable. And in this respect, he saw Montgomery as a microcosm of the national problem.

At the same time, there was a growing trend of black migration from rural areas to urban centres. The experiences of black soldiers in the two world wars, the years of the Great Depression and the growing popularity and increasing use of the motor car all contributed to this process. The result was that African-Americans gained economically, made new contacts, adopted a broader outlook and grasped opportunities for educational advancement.

Taken together, King sensed that these factors had imbued African-Americans with their new sense of self and hope. America was theirs too and nothing less than full citizenship would be acceptable. This was the attitude of the 'New Negro', as King described fellow-campaigners in the South.[67]

By this time, King had broadened his argument for civil rights. Crucially, he realised that to achieve real freedom in the United States African-Americans needed the right to vote. He believed that the denial of this right was at the root of many problems in the South.

In an effort to move the Federal Government to grant the ballot, 37,000 black and white Americans attended a 'Prayer Pilgrimage' which was held on 17 May 1957. They assembled at the Lincoln Memorial in Washington DC to commemorate the third anniversary of the Supreme Court ruling against segregation in public schools.

At the gathering, King urged the president and Congress to give the ballot to African-Americans, because it was their fundamental right.[68] He criticised the legislative branch of government as being hypocritical, and said that both political parties had *betrayed the cause of justice*. He chastised politicians as men prone to having a *high blood pressure of words and an anaemia of deeds*.

Soldiers, battles, war, victory were all part of the armoury of words that King employed in his crusade in the summer of 1957. Its aim was the implementation of a new educational and action programme in the South that would make voting rights for African-Americans a reality.

Meanwhile, the demand for King's services as a preacher and speaker continued. The success of his speech at the Prayer Pilgrimage had an extraordinary effect. He was the recipient of honorary degrees from many prestigious institutions, including Morehouse College, which granted him an honorary doctorate. In bestowing the award, President Benjamin Mays said of his former pupil: 'You are mature beyond your years, wiser at twenty-eight than most men at sixty; more courageous in a righteous struggle than most men can ever be; living a faith that most men worry themselves into nameless graves when here and there a great soul forgets himself into immortality.'[69]

*

By early 1958, King had finished his book *Stride To Freedom*, a first-hand account of the Montgomery bus boycott. About this time, James Lawson, who was FOR's organiser in Nashville, teamed up with Glenn Smiley and Ralph Abernathy, holding workshops and speaking at various venues. They also produced *Martin Luther King and the Montgomery Story*. Through the successful distribution of this comic book (a quarter of a million copies were sold) the *Montgomery Story* and the power of non-violence had spread to the grassroots. Reinforcing this message were the distribution of two brochures entitled: 'The Power of Nonviolence' and 'How to Practice Nonviolence'.

In September, King went to New York City to promote *Stride to Freedom*. While he was signing books at Blumstein's in Harlem, a woman called out to him: 'Are you Martin Luther King?'

'Yes', King replied.

The woman plunged a letter opener into King's chest with such force that the instrument was lodged dangerously close to his aorta. His doctor later told him he would have died if he had sneezed.

When King spoke to the press at the hospital ten days later, he said he bore no ill-will towards his attacker Mrs Izola Curry. He then made a chilling statement to the press about the stabbing which he said demonstrated that a *climate of hatred and bitterness* was all-pervasive in America which, in turn, bred lawlessness.[70]

If there was a good side to the incident, it was the sympathy King received from a wide cross-section of Americans. Among the many letters he received, was a note from a white high school student who had read of his suffering and declared: 'I'm so happy you did not sneeze.'[71]

Did the attack deter him? To many observers, King seemed unusually calm after the attempt on his life. This external appearance, he attributed solely to his faith and to the power of God. Though uncertain, he saw his future as *promising*.

King was patient about getting back to work, and he spent a lot of time thinking about himself and his mission. He had not the slightest intention of halting his progress. If anything, the attack strengthened his belief that God had chosen him to lead his people. King felt that both he and Coretta were preparing themselves for a more challenging task which would mean enduring persecution and suffering. The only way forward was through re-dedicating themselves to non-violence.[72]

Journey to India

During his convalescence, King thought a great deal about going to India. Two years earlier, in 1956, Jawaharlal Nehru, the Indian prime minister, had visited the US and expressed his wish to meet King. The meeting never took place, but the intention was strong on both sides that King should visit India.

For King, there was a greater sense of urgency to do so now. As the victim of violence, he felt the Gandhian message of civil disobedience – employed so successfully in the Montgomery boycott – merited closer study.

King asked Coretta and his friend Dr Reddick to accompany him. While Coretta was interested in the women of India, Dr Reddick was a student of India and King's biographer. On this visit, what may have escaped King's notice, he hoped his companions would pick up.

When the Kings arrived in India, they regarded themselves as pilgrims, not as tourists. The reception that greeted them was *grand* and, at last, King met Nehru. King was surprised to be recognised by many among the crowds that had flocked to see him.

On this tour, time was always short and the Kings were constantly having to move on. While the question of colour was common to both King and millions of Indians, the *strongest bond of fraternity* was the common cause of minority and colonial peoples in America, Africa and Asia, determined to free themselves from racism and imperialism.

The observant preacher King took in everything. Indians

were *keen* on the *race problem* and wherever he spoke or lectured the gathering was usually large. They particularly enjoyed the Negro Spirituals sung by Coretta. He praised the Indian press, especially for their *better continuity* of the Montgomery bus boycott than their American counterparts. In India's largest cities, King found during his chats with newspapermen that their editorials were well-informed of the burning issues around the world.[73]

If India's physical size impressed King, its *vast problems* of overcrowded cities, high unemployment, homelessness and poverty humbled him. He was surprised by the low crime rate, which he regarded as *another concrete manifestation of the wonderful spiritual quality of the Indian people*. The Kings visited many places associated with Gandhi as well as ashrams, temples and village communities, so important in the subcontinent. They joined in worship as the texts of the sacred scriptures of Hindus, Christians, Jews, Muslims and Buddhists were read, a reflection of Gandhi's recognition of a multi-faith approach to God.[74]

King travelled to the ashram where Gandhi had embarked on his historic non-violent Salt March, a momentous trek to the sea to collect salt in protest against a government monopoly. He recalled the Mahatma's unrivalled achievement through mobilising and inspiring a larger number of people than any other person. Gandhi did so, King said, with love, understanding, goodwill and strong opposition to evil legislation. Taken together, he was able to weaken and defeat British imperialism. Of this, King felt convinced that it was *one of the most significant things that ever happened in the history of the world*.

King found the Indians supportive of the American experiment with non-violence and being there reinforced his belief in the non-violent movement. He understood that in its truest sense, non-violent resistance does not equate an *unrealistic submission to evil power* but was founded on a collective identity that developed when a group has the shared experience of being on the receiving end of violence and bitterness. Why was this so? Because the inflicted *may develop a sense of shame in the opponent and thereby bring about a transformation and change of heart.*[75]

King took a particular interest in 'Untouchability'. The untouchables faced a grim reality: they were the lowest of the low in India's rigid hierarchal caste system yet were the hardest workers. The Untouchables were the marginalised and downtrodden members of society, whose birth condemned them to a life of penury as menial labourers, scavengers, skinners of the holy cow and handlers of human excrement.

King compared the plight of the Untouchables to that of his own people. Years later, he would recall that before he spoke to students in south India, he was introduced as a fellow Untouchable from the United States of America. The shock he felt at being referred to as *Untouchable* heightened his awareness of his own dilemma: the 20 million African-Americans who were corralled in an *airtight cage of poverty* in an affluent country. This huge number of people inhabited disgraceful slums and their children attended sub-standard schools. Such considerations confirmed what he confided to himself: *Yes, I am an Untouchable, and every Negro in the United States of America is an Untouchable.*[76]

Overall, what King learned about India was that diversity was the key – a variety of peoples, religions, cultures, problems, contrasts and achievements. By the time of his departure, he was convinced that non-violent resistance was the best weapon of an oppressed people in its struggle for freedom. He marvelled at the *amazing results* of the movement in India and noted that *hatred and bitterness* did not normally follow non-violent campaigns.[77]

And so ended King's *marvellous* Indian journey, experiences which he said would remain dear to him as long as the *chords of memory shall lengthen*. With such thoughts still fresh in his mind, just a few days after his return to Montgomery, King preached a sermon on Gandhi.

The world doesn't like people like Gandhi. That's strange, isn't it? They don't like people like Christ; they don't like people like Lincoln. They killed him, this man who had done all that for India, who gave his life and who mobilized and galvanised 400 million people for Independence.

He went on to review non-violence, love, hate and history. Gandhi was shot and died on a Friday, the same day that Christ died, but that wasn't the end of the story. Good Friday, King reminded his audience, was not the end but the beginning. In effect, Gandhi was shot *into the hearts of humanity*. In composing this sermon, King recalled that like Abraham Lincoln, Gandhi also belonged *to the Ages*.[78]

Towards the end of the 1950s, King's reputation grew. His appeal was not confined to Africans and Indians, for now conservative white Americans were beginning to see him as attractive. Why? In answering this question, one biographer, Adam Fairclough has compared King's soaring prestige to the fate of two other black leaders: Paul Robeson and W E B DuBois.

Paul Robeson, the internationally renowned singer, actor and a life-long civil rights activist was engaged in left-wing politics. Amid the tensions of the Cold War, Robeson spoke out against American foreign policy. By urging African-Americans not to fight on America's side should there be a war with the Soviet Union, the former highly-regarded 'Great American' swiftly and dramatically became 'un-American': his passport was withdrawn, his concerts disrupted and cancelled, he appeared before Congressional committees and the FBI shadowed him. Thus, Robeson's brilliant career was destroyed.

DuBois was the leading black intellectual of the 20th century and a founding member of the NAACP. He too had socialist/communist sympathies and was dealt with similarly by the American establishment. After joining the Communist Party in 1957, he moved to Ghana, where he lived until his death in

W E B DuBois (1868–1963) was an eminent African-American sociologist and activist. DuBois challenged the logic of Booker T Washington and argued that change could come only with agitation and protest. Later, he became the early leader of the Pan-Africanist movement, which focused on gaining independence for African nations and cultivating unity among black people throughout the world.

1963. In a country steeped in Cold War intrigue and tensions, King appeared to be a much more acceptable black American leader. At this time, King was not overtly political. His activities and pronouncements aimed at reforms were gradual and limited, bounded and founded upon the essential principles of Americanism: the Constitution, the Declaration of Independence, the Christian way of life and the 'American Dream'. So, unlike Robeson and DuBois, King did not invoke socialist principles to justify his struggle.

At this time, there was nothing radical about King's programme. He carried none of the *class conscious socialist-oriented radicalism* of the 1930s and 1940s. As *Time* magazine put it, King's 'conservative' leadership was reflected in the clothes he wore; no wonder black radicals were scathing of his seemingly simplistic political stance. And his acceptance by powerful whites aroused further suspicion that he might be a 'tool' to be used by the elite.

In any case, the truth was that times had changed and so did elements of the American power structure. With postwar decolonisation, racism was discredited and increasingly being replaced by 'reforms'. Thus, the rigid hierarchy of the South was challenged by the reforming policy outlawing racial discrimination, as stated in *Brown v. Board of Education*, a Supreme Court ruling that declared segregation in schools illegal.[79] Nonetheless, the historical process was not that straightforward.

While powerful sections of the white elite were for reform, others were not. It was from this paradoxical situation that King was able to play upon the conscience of those whites who were susceptible to change. Indeed, it was argued that were it not for their willingness, the civil rights movement would have been less successful and King's efforts completely nullified.

In other words, King was not as pliable as it had seemed at first. Politically, he had done his homework and, for now, his political advisers Bayard Rustin – one of King's collaborators and earliest advisers – and Levison were at one with him. The political realities of the time dictated that it was pragmatic for the civil rights movement to adopt an evolutionary, rather than a revolutionary approach. King's independence of mind and self-criticism enabled the movement to exploit the latitude that a non-partisan, non-political strategy allowed.[80]

Sit-ins and politics

On 29 November 1959, King announced to his congregation that he would be leaving the Dexter Avenue Baptist Church. In his farewell message, he said he was pressed towards the mainstream by the *rolling tides of historical necessity*: his work-load had tripled and, as a consequence, he was trying to do much more than he could. Instead of a lessening after the boycott, his responsibilities – and the pressures on him – grew.

To build upon what had been achieved, he felt he would be more effective by moving to Atlanta to become co-pastor of the Ebenezer Baptist Church and be nearer the offices of the SCLC in Atlanta. The time was right, he told the press, to launch an all-out offensive against segregation in all its forms. To this end, both the young and the old had to be trained in the ways of non-violent resistance. He was now concerned with *new methods* of struggle which included involvement of the masses.[81]

It is just as well that King was now becoming more involved for early in 1960, four black students at North Carolina A and T College triggered a new phase in the civil rights struggle. At the lunch counter of a Woolworth's department store in Greensboro where they had been denied service, they started a sit-in. They were joined by others, including many white sympathisers, mostly students. By 8 February the sit-ins had reached Durham and Winston-Salem. Within a week, the action had affected Charlotte, Elizabeth City, Raleigh, Fayetteville, Norfolk and Portsmouth, Rock Hill and Virginia, South Carolina. As it spread further to include North Carolina and other states, a few young men, such as the Rev Douglas Moore and the Rev James Lawson emerged as leaders.

Before the sit-ins were two weeks old, King went to Durham to meet Rev Moore. After a tour of the city he reminded the student leader that the main thrust of the struggle was 'justice versus justice, not black against white.' Openness towards whites was fundamental as was the message 'jail, not bail.'

King urged the young activists to organise a Coordinating Council that would bring together the different groups in the various cities. When the council was formed, predictably, there was keen rivalry for the leadership positions from those who supported the NAACP, CORE and the SCLC. Interestingly, there were many who felt that the Council and its sit-ins should continue to be 'student-led.'

Overall, the sit-ins caught the imagination of students across the South and elsewhere. By March 1960, there were sit-ins in more than 50 cities. Crucially, all were underscored by the philosophy of non-violence.[82] Thereafter, Ella Baker had persuaded the SCLC to hold a national conference of sit-in delegates, which was attended by over 200 activists on 15 April 1960. As one of the keynote speakers, King suggested the formation of an organisation devoted to student action. Thus, the Student Nonviolent Coordinating Committee was created. Thereafter, student activists pressed their claims in an unprecedented surge of activities.

The protests had bred a new spirit in the movement which, in turn, led to widespread discussion on college campuses. Throughout, King commended the students for having followed the road of non-violence. The moral obligation on the part of campaigners/protesters was to press home the wrongness of segregation, not to alienate white colleagues. Thus the *ultimate aim* of King and his followers during the protest was to be reconciled with *our white brothers*.

The student movement represented a shift in the manner in which African-American protest was conducted. Instead of patiently awaiting lumbering, long-drawn out legal submissions, direct action was preferred. Thus, the seeming patience of an older generation contrasted sharply with younger people who were unwilling to wait any longer to exercise their basic rights as American citizens.

That year 1960 King was arrested and charged with falsifying his Alabama state income tax returns. This marked a turning point in the freedom struggle.[83] By now, King had become a national figure and as such, white Southerners targeted him and his offence as being serious enough to lead to a ten-year imprisonment. He sensed this and recorded his fears as, once more, he faced an all-white Southern jury. The atmosphere was tense and the outcome seemed inevitable. But King survived the legal onslaught because of the wise counsel of his able representatives. The Jury acquitted him.

The lesson of this battle, arising from an *offence* that should never have been brought to court was not lost on King. Polite and grateful as he was to Messrs Ming and Delaney, he wished such legal services as they had provided for him were available for the tens of thousands of black civil rights workers and their families, ordinary people who were tried every day in *prejudiced* courtrooms.[84]

In New York on 23 June 1960, King met Senator John F Kennedy for the first time. Given King's critical view of the Federal Government, during the one-hour meeting he was frank and honest. He was impressed with Kennedy who showed a keen interest in civil rights. But despite the Senator's familiarity with, and promise to tackle the question of the right to vote, King had doubts. He was convinced that Kennedy lacked a full understanding of the extent of the problem. He did not deny Kennedy's

King and civil rights leaders meet President Kennedy at the White House

intellectual commitment to integration, it was his emotional involvement that was at issue. Nonetheless, should Kennedy become President, privately King was inclined to believe that Kennedy would do the *right thing*.

As the Presidential campaign progressed, many of King's friends suggested that he should declare his support for Kennedy. But King stood firm on a point of principle which he had spelt out to the Senator when they met: that he was unwilling to endorse any candidate publicly, and could not envisage a time when his view on this would change.[85]

Later, in October 1960, King joined the sit-ins in Atlanta which he felt was a moral obligation. Within a few days, he and over 280 students were arrested. They were all released, except King who was charged with violating his probation, arising from an earlier charge of still carrying an Alabama driver's license when he was stopped by police in De Kalb County. Consequently, he was held in Fulton County Jail and then taken to De Kalb County

Jail where he was chained to the floor. Then at about three in the morning, he was woken and taken to Reidsville State Prison, where he endured *mental anguish* that arose from a combination of not knowing the destination of his journey, being denied food and the sheer uselessness and waste of time just waiting around, all because of a mere traffic violation.[86]

When the African-American community found out that King was being held, there was uproar. Even while he was in the Fulton County Jail, there were people who urged both Nixon and Kennedy to take some action. Now in Reidsville, despite his reputation (or perhaps because of it), King was thrown among a rag-bag of hardened criminals. The contrast could not be sharper. This was an entirely new and awkward situation for the learned, prominent, middle-class preacher.

Cell-bound, King was worried about his pregnant wife. He called, then wrote to Coretta about his separation from her and his children. He hoped, even in her condition, that she would visit him, and made it clear how very badly he had wanted to see her and the children.[87]

With the approach of the 1960 Presidential election, the US could no longer ignore the Civil Rights struggle. As it was, King's incarceration had aroused much diplomatic activity at the highest levels of US politics. The two contenders for the Presidency adopted different stances on the question of King's imprisonment. Nixon made no comment regardless of the dangers that King's isolation presented, while Kennedy thought there was something he could do. He telephoned Mrs. King and offered his assistance. After the intervention of the Senator's campaign manager and brother Robert Kennedy, King was released on a $2,000 bond.[88] This act, whether or not it was politically-inspired, was well-received by King's father, who declared his support for Kennedy in the Presidential race. King, on the other hand, was not willing to endorse either candidate.[89]

Why was King so cagey about publicly supporting Senator Kennedy? Although he thought that of the two presidential candidates, Kennedy would have made the 'best' president, King remained neutral, impartial, non-partisan. His father though, was more committed.

King addressing a student rally at Birmingham, Alabama, 1960

IMPARTIALITY 63

From Albany to Birmingham

In the spring of 1961, the sit-ins were taken on the road in the form of Freedom Rides that were organised by CORE and aimed at dramatizing the lack of compliance among Southern institutions with long-standing Court orders and other rulings banning segregation in interstate travel.

Freedom Riders in the South boarded Greyhound buses and were well aware of the dangers they faced. Indeed, many of them were beaten by white gangs; and in spite of arrests, no one was charged or jailed. 'The specific intention of the Freedom Ride was to create a crisis,' the activist James Farmer wrote. 'We were counting on the bigots in the South to do our work for us.'

Feeling among African-Americans was so strong that even the violence could not stop their march. On the evening of 20 May, as King spoke to hundreds of people in Ralph Abernathy's church, an angry mob surrounded it and hurled missiles at the windows. They laid siege to the building through the night, until the governor of Alabama called in the National Guard to defuse a potentially dangerous situation.

By the autumn, the persistent campaign and pressure exerted by the Freedom Riders had begun to have an effect. Signs from the Interstate Commerce Commission appeared on buses and at bus stations declaring discrimination on the grounds of race, colour and creed illegal.[90]

A year and a half after King had moved back to Atlanta, his wife and some of his close associates observed a few changes in him. For one thing, the once proud dresser had become less concerned about clothes and his appearance. Coretta was especially struck by this but noted a much bigger change that had overtaken her husband: greater evidence of his selflessness. Coretta noted that he was both more relaxed and more reserved since their trip to India. Above all, he was more ready than ever to carry the huge responsibilities of his leadership role.

King was conscious of these changes. He admitted that he had become *more serious*, but to prevent giving the wrong impression he was quick to assure those near and dear to him that he had not lost his sense of humour. *I know I've let many opportunities go by without using it,* he said. *I seldom joke in my speeches anymore. I forget to.*

His public persona was of a reserved figure. The burden of leadership now weighed heavily and could not be disguised. The growing demands of public leadership left little time for his family responsibilities as father and husband. When Coretta sought his interest in deciding which school Yoki should attend, he delegated the full responsibility to her. 'All of that selflessness might be commendable in a famous public figure,' as one biographer remarked, 'but King's version brought no pleasure to his family.'[91]

Towards the end of 1961, W G Anderson, leader of the Albany Movement in south-west Georgia, invited King to assist them. Many people in this

King greeted at Atlanta airport by Coretta, Yolanda and Martin Luther III 1960

community were keen to start a voter registration drive. They needed to kick-start their campaign which explained King's presence there. In turn, he welcomed the arrival of Freedom Riders in Albany in December 1961 as bearers of the non-violent campaign. Clearly their presence in that community would serve to expose the lack of respect and injustices that African-Americans had to confront as inter-state travellers in the South.

Dr. Anderson's invitation to King was timely. With a population of some 27,000 African-Americans, the Albany movement prepared itself for the struggle against segregation. Unlike other cities in the South, here non-violent protest went beyond sit-ins to include jail-ins, sit-ins, wide-ins, in conjunction with other political action, including boycotts and legal challenges that were employed in places where discrimination was practised.

The protests were proving to be more effective than the city authorities had expected and the SCLC gave its full support to the Albany movement, both morally and financially. On 16 December 1961, the movement began in earnest when many of the city's citizens were jailed. King was among them. He was charged with 'parading without a permit', with causing a disturbance and for obstruction. When he had arrived in Albany, the idea of being jailed had not been on his mind; he had not expected to stay longer than a day or two in the city before returning home. The situation was volatile and King acted as he saw fit.

On the night when the arrested black citizens were finally released, King addressed them at a mass meeting. He was overwhelmed by their commitment and dignity. Some months later in July 1962, King was again convicted for leading an earlier protest. Seeing cells overcrowded with women of advanced age, teenagers and the middle aged left an indelible impression upon King. Thereafter, Albany was engulfed in turmoil and members of the business community urged city officials to reach a settlement. The agreement, subsequently made was, however, dishonoured by local officials. This prompted retaliatory action from determined non-violent protesters, and so the protest was resumed.[92]

While he was imprisoned, King had begun to write his *Jail Diary* in which he described his *filthy* cell as being home. Coretta visited him twice before returning to Atlanta. Soon after, he wrote in his *Diary* that he and other inmates held morning and evening services, and though he could not see the other prisoners (some of whom were white) he could clearly hear them singing.

In this worst of jails, King's endurance was tested. He was relieved from the claustrophobia by his visit to the courtroom where he had the opportunity to see Coretta, friends and associates who were maintaining the campaign. Later, his father visited him and he was happy that his mother understood and was supportive of the difficult part he was playing in Albany.

He had learned about President Kennedy's interest in talking to African-American leaders and was so impressed by Kennedy's forthrightness that he immediately sent a message of appreciation to him. What King said was simple and direct: he urged Kennedy to continue to apply the full moral authority of his Presidency to alleviate a *critical situation*.

The long-awaited day came when King was visited by his children, Yolanda, Martin Luther III and Dexter. After five weeks, seeing them for less than half an hour lifted his spirits.

About this time, he was working on a new book and had written three sermons in jail, all dealing with the Christian gospel's relevance to the social and economic life of man and all of which he had preached before: 'A Tender Heart and A Tough Mind', 'Love in Action' and 'Loving Your Enemies'.

As the trial continued, on the last day (8 August) King and Abernathy testified. King said it was a sickening experience during which he was twice attended by a doctor for exhaustion. Eventually, he received a suspended sentence and wrote that he was not entirely surprised, though he maintained that the sentence was *unjust*. He and Abernathy had decided to adopt the strategy of calling-off the marches which would give the Commission an opportunity to save face and thus demonstrate *good faith* on the part of the Albany movement.[93]

Reflecting on the Albany campaign, he found himself questioning his leadership of the civil rights movement. If he had to do it again, he said, he would 'guide' the black community's leadership differently. He identified weaknesses, responsibility for which he attributed to each one who had participated. Being human meant there were no magic buttons to press to mobilise for the best results. He felt that the struggle had lost the initiative and he blamed himself for not being wiser at the time. Why? Because they had targeted the political apparatus instead of the economic power structure. The inappropriateness of the diffuse approach of his leadership had become painfully clear to King. Such a strategy which aimed the protest at segregation generally, instead of being more focused on a particular facet, was a mistake. His followers deserved better, he thought. He regretted their depression and despair.

In King's view, the Albany experience was beneficial because making mistakes was part of the learning process. Moreover, the young people there were now stronger. King claimed that Albany was a partial victory; not the end but a beginning.[94]

The Birmingham Campaign

In 1963, Birmingham, Alabama was unlike any other part of the South. An industrial city steeped in wealth, shady deals and corruption among its industrialists and trade unions, it was also a bastion of segregation.[95] In this tense, volatile environment, it was unlikely that human rights and justice for African-Americans would prevail. Fear permeated all walks of life and for King, this landscape was a catalyst for the civil rights movement. A more imposing challenge would have been hard to find. And amid all this, on 28 March, the Kings' fourth child, Bernice Albertine was born. Once again, the proud father was overjoyed but he was dismayed that his private life was being subsumed by his public responsibilities.

King described the city as being *trapped for decades in a Rip van Winkle slumber*, a city whose respected officials and leaders were apparently oblivious of history, the Founding Fathers, the American Constitution and the Supreme Court's 1954 decision, which outlawed segregation in public schools. Here, the brutalisation of African-Americans was a given.

Presiding over this state of affairs were Eugene 'Bull' Connor, the police commissioner – who had recently thrown his hat in the ring to become the city's mayor – and Governor George Wallace. Both held racist views which depended on the continued oppression of African-Americans.

In Birmingham, one of the leading figures of the movement was the Reverend Fred Shuttlesworth who had organised the Alabama Christian Movement for Human Rights in 1956, a group determined to counteract racist attacks and lobby for human rights when the NAACP was legally harassed and closed down in Alabama. He knew well of the terror of Connor's racism. The commissioner spoke regularly at Citizen's Council meetings, exploiting racial tensions to defeat a reformist incumbent.

The SCLC gave its support to Shuttlesworth and the ACMHR. But while the approach was familiar – sit-ins, boycotts, protests – breaking down segregation in Birmingham was no walk-over. If anything, as King predicted, it was likely to be the 'toughest' fight that the civil rights movement had had to face. Why? Because a victory in Birmingham, King hoped, could mean not only striking a blow at the heart of segregation in America, but would also add immeasurably to the momentum of the movement. This campaign, as he saw it, was an opportunity to learn the lessons of Albany, which meant being less general and more particular in directing the protest concentratedly, effectively against 'one aspect' of the evil and complex web that was the system of segregation.

King and his co-leaders confronted Birmingham's race relations problem with 'Project C'. The SCLC and ACMHR representatives met in room 30 at the Gaston Motel, the venue for all their future strategy sessions. The signs were good: over 200 people had pledged their support for the demonstrations, declaring their readiness to spend up to five days in jail. Hopes were high.

But then news reached King of an impending mayoral election because no candidate in the last contest, which included Connor and the moderate, Alfred Boutwell, had a clear majority. As it was, the 'run off' to come would have disrupted the planned Civil Rights protest. King felt that it was best for him and all the SCLC staff to leave Birmingham for the duration of the election, but he feared losing contact with the courageous volunteers. The reasoning behind this decision was that while King and his followers' hoped that Connor would be defeated, they wanted to avoid the campaign being used as a 'political football'.

Performer and activist Harry Belafonte

In other cities, supporters were being rallied to the cause. In New York, Harry Belafonte, the singer, actor and SCLC supporter, called together a group of wealthy New Yorkers in his apartment to hear King and Shuttlesworth speak. Above all, the pair asked for money to fund bail bonds and, there and then, a committee was formed and money collected.

Immediately after the election, King and his staff flew back to Birmingham. The day after his return, the direct action campaign was launched in Birmingham.

Following Albert Boutwell's victory in the mayoral election, the *Birmingham News* headlined the dawning of a 'New Day'. For King and supporters of the civil rights movement, it was indeed a 'new day' but of a different kind. The campaign started well with sit-ins and regular mass meetings, the cumulative effect of which reinforced the community's self-belief.[96] The mass meetings featured rousing freedom songs which King called the *soul* of the movement.

At the end of these meetings, Abernathy, Shuttleworth and King would take turns in appealing for volunteers to join their non-violent army. A prerequisite for such recruits was the capacity to absorb violence without retaliating. King's crusade was to spare nothing in the attempt to bring people together for the goal of social change. But certain facts could not be denied: there was clear division that had to be bridged, especially the fact that he was perceived as an 'outsider' during the early days

> Harry Belafonte was the son of immigrants from Martinique and Jamaica. One of the first black entertainers to make it in Hollywood, he first achieved fame with calypso-style songs, including Day-O (Banana Boat Song) and Jamaica Farewell. Throughout the 1960s and 1970s, however, he was also an prominent campaigner in the civil rights movement. He was there on the famous Selma to Montgomery March and he was there in Atlanta for the funeral of King.

of this campaign. Nonetheless, that low point was transcended as King found new inspiration to transform the negative feelings and misunderstandings he found towards him and other 'outsiders' into renewed belief. His heartfelt appeals won enough support for him to reflect and reiterate what had by now become a recurring message: that there was among his followers a 'new unity,' that nothing could stop the regenerated feelings of empowerment that would arise from the foundation of the doomed old order so callously presided over by racists such as Bull Connor.

Amid all the bigotry, hatred and political violence that surrounded him in Birmingham, King said he felt he had arrived at the point for which he had been preparing all his life. And when his lawyer arrived from New York with news that Harry Belafonte had indeed raised sufficient bail funds for those who would be arrested, King felt a great sense of relief. Once more, at a critical juncture in his life, darkness was overcome by light.[97]

The Letter from Jail

In the days that followed, the campaign was characterised by sit-ins as the main form of direct-action, sustained crucially by regular night-time mass meetings, the centrepiece of which were King's electrifying speeches and sermons. The people listened to him with a mixture of reverence and excitement. He was like no one else they had ever known. To the majority of the protesters he was no longer an 'outsider.' And in the charged atmosphere of these gatherings, music filled the air and enriched the soul. These 'freedom songs' stirred many who were weary, infusing in them great hope as they prepared for the coming of the new day. Indeed as King led the thousands of marchers to downtown Birmingham, the police allowed them to walk further than ever. They sang as they marched and soon enough Connor ordered his men to apprehend the trespassers in the inner sanctum of his city. The jail capacity could not accommodate all the protesters, so Connor's police grabbed the ring-leaders, King and Abernathy.

Predictably, King found himself once more in jail. Though each time was different, he would never forget the morning after he was locked away in solitary confinement. In a newspaper that was 'slipped' to him, he read an article endorsed by eight clergymen. They were direct in their criticism of the extremist demonstrators who disregarded law and order. The more King read of what these pious men had written, the more upset he became. He felt he had no choice, but to respond.

So, he began writing a letter from the Birmingham jail on scraps of paper passed to him by a friendly African-American prison guard and concluded it on a pad that his attorney had given to him. Addressing the signatories as *My Dear Fellow Clergymen*, King responded immediately to the charge that his non-violent campaign activities were *unwise* and *untimely*. With so little time at his disposal, he said he rarely responded to criticism of his work and ideas. Indeed, if he had tried to answer all the criticism that they had made it would be far too time-consuming and unconstructive. Nonetheless he felt bound to respond, and said so in his 'Letter.'

King took issue with the notion that 'outsiders' were streaming into Birmingham. He denied this and explained his presence in Birmingham simply: he was there because he was President of the SCLC and, more importantly, because of intolerable injustice in Birmingham. Using ethical and democratic principles as his guide, King pronounced upon the *raison d'être*, the whys and wherefores of the civil rights revolt. He told his fellow-Christians about the journey he had made from his home to Birmingham. He said he had brought with him the gospel of freedom, much as the Apostle Paul had done during his time. For good measure, he referred to the connectedness of the myriad communities of the

South and the many states of the country and within which no one should be considered an 'outsider.'[98] *Injustice anywhere is a threat to justice everywhere*, he argued. *We are caught in an inescapable network of mutuality, tied in the single garment of destiny. Whatever affects one directly affects all indirectly.*[99]

He rejected the charge that the civil rights demonstrations were deplorable by turning the argument on its head. Their statement failed to show a similar concern for the conditions that were responsible for such actions. He felt sure that none of these religious leaders would accept anything less than a full analysis of both the effects and underlying causes. In other words, while the Birmingham demonstrations were unfortunate, the more important point was that the city's white power structure left the African-American community with no choice.

Why direct-action? King was frank. He explained that the purpose was to use the crisis-packed situation to bring the opposing sides to the negotiating table. He agreed with the clergymen's preference for negotiation but reminded them that the time had come for the beloved South to discard the tragic barrenness of *monologue* and replace it with a dialogue that achieved tangible results.

King then addressed another of the God-fearing signatories' gripes: that the action taken by him and the campaigners was untimely. He repeated a message he had delivered at different times, in different places. Freedom, he said, was never granted by the oppressor; it had to be fought for by the oppressed. And, he added, there was an unmistakeable urgency about the direct-action campaign against segregation. Already justice for Africans-Americans, *too long delayed*, in effect, meant *justice denied*.[100] He cited the bombings of black churches and homes, and the indignities attending segregation in the city's stores. He reminded the clergymen of efforts, made in good faith by the demonstrators' leaders to negotiate, that were stubbornly ignored. And why were these moderate men so alarmed by the actions of the oppressed?

Why did they not distinguish what was fair and what was unfair in law? The Bible was clear about this distinction: King quoted St. Augustine as saying that an 'unjust law is no law at all.' History was replete with examples of the poor and oppressed disobeying kings, emperors and dictators who maintained their oppressive rule through 'legal' means. Hitler had acted 'legally' in his treatment of the Jews, while they, in turn, acted 'illegally' when they tried to flee from the tyranny of legal persecution. In like manner, African- Americans were perceived as acting 'illegally,' when they opposed unjust laws such as the vicious segregation statutes. By so doing, were they wrong? Or were they, as King put it, redefining their status in terms of a higher law that was acceptable to people of goodwill.[101]

King also addressed the pace of social change. He compared the jet-like speed with which the peoples of Africa and Asia were moving towards political independence, while African-Americans still crept along very slowly in their quest to be served at a local lunch counter. There were limits to the patience of an oppressed people. And yet, he pointed out that his detractors should not speak of the Birmingham campaign as 'extreme' for it was unrealistic to oppress people forever. For those who were denied expression of their civil rights, there was encouragement that it was the zeitgeist as peoples of Africa, Asia, the Caribbean and Americans fought to be socially, economically and politically free. Framed within this international context, King saw African-Americans as moving with great speed toward the *promised land of racial justice.*

King was caught between two opposing forces within the African-American community — the forces of complacency and of bitterness and hatred. His concern was not emulation of the 'do-nothingness' endemic among the complacent or the hatred and despair of the black power advocates, but rather to engage in peaceful protest informed by love and non-violence.

While some of his 'white brothers' in the South were supportive of the truth of the civil rights campaign, he felt bound to express his disappointment with the Church not because he was an unhelpful critic, but someone who was nurtured in the bosom of the Church.[102]

When King first came to Birmingham, he was hopeful that the city's white religious leaders would recognise the African-Americans' cause. He was saddened by what he found. The Civil Rights Movement had never received the much-needed co-operation of the Church. But though he wept over the Church's casual attitude he assured the clergymen that the tears he shed were tears of love for *there can be no deep disappointment where there is not deep Love*. But, he scrawled, *how we have blemished and scarred that body through social neglect and through fear of being nonconformists*.[103]

He explained why his letter was so long. He hoped that there would be nothing in it that either overstated the truth or reflected unreasonable impatience. And, as always, his aim was nothing less than brotherhood.

In conclusion, King appealed to the clergymen to view the Civil Rights Movement as integral to the American dream and predicted that one day the South would come to know its *real heroes*: the young students and ministers of the church and old women. He envisioned a South that would no longer be divided, but united.[104]

When he had completed this unusual letter, King got it out of his cell in bits, to a member of his staff. Soon after, on 19 April King and Abernathy were released on bond. King accepted his release from jail for two reasons. First, because of his separation from the activists, he felt the need to quickly reconnect with the SCLC leadership to deal with the numerous cases of contempt of court. Second, because he needed to implement a new phase of the campaign which would lead to a speedy victory.

So far, King had experienced a great deal and we should remember that he was just 34 years old, as he prepared to lead a march from the New Pilgrim Baptist Church to the Birmingham City jail. Over 5,000 people had gathered, but they could not proceed because Police Commissioner Connor and his forces of law and order (armed with fire trucks and water hoses) had blocked the road. Unarmed citizens were now confronted with brute force. The outcome was, for the majority of observers, not in doubt: blood on police officers' hands seemed a foregone conclusion. But they were wrong, for after the marchers had kneeled at the roadside and prayed and sang, as if fortified, they rose to the call of a minister among them to walk on towards the phalanx of policemen, firemen and their hoses. The situation was extremely tense, as the marchers moved closer. Then, an amazing thing happened: Connor's men stood by as the marchers passed by them. There was no effort to stop them. Thus, the powerless were empowered, an *unarmed love overcoming armed hatred*. King was moved, as never before.[105]

It was King's conviction that the involvement of students was integral to the campaign's success. Strategically, they would add a new dimension that would be beneficial to all age groups, but most importantly it gave young people a sense that they had a vital contribution to make in winning freedom and justice.[106]

Recruiting the youth was a strategic masterstroke. As staff members welcomed them, there was an urgency among them to learn more and to join the freedom movement. To the protests raised in the major media, King was quick to respond. *Where were the media gurus in centuries past when segregation misused and abused African-American children?*

King was delighted with Birmingham's youth which reminded him of a moment during the Montgomery bus protest when an elderly woman was asked why she had become involved. She was doing it for her children and grandchildren, she said. Just a few years later, in Birmingham many of the city's children and grandchildren *were doing it for themselves*.[107]

King had no doubt that in the confrontation to come the Civil Rights Movement would win. At a mass meeting, he spoke about his fellow-campaigners' historic mission: *There are those who write history. There are those who make history. There are those who experience history...you are certainly experiencing history. And you will make it possible for historians of the future to write a marvellous chapter. Never in the history of this nation have so many people been arrested for the cause of freedom and human dignity.*[108]

On 7 May, thousands marched through town singing songs of freedom. This moving sight astounded the local business elite for whom, it seemed, the writing was already on the wall. In the negotiations that followed, an agreement was announced. Was this agreement the solution to the Birmingham crisis? This was the question as news flashed around the world. Or was it cause for new fears? Predictably, white extremists were unhappy and decided to act in the only way they knew how: by resisting with violence. The home of Alfred, King's brother, and the Gaston Motel were bombed. But such incendiary devices were not enough to prevent the signing of the agreement which marked the end of a protracted campaign for rights and human dignity. King was thankful to all Americans who had contributed to the expression of solidarity with African-Americans. At this point, though Birmingham was not magically transformed into a desegregated city, it had taken the crucial first step which, King hoped, would eventually make it a model of race relations.[109]

Soon enough, there was movement towards this hope. Birmingham's success was approved of by both President Kennedy and his brother Robert, the Attorney-General. In turn, this had the effect of quickening the momentum towards civil rights legislation.

Against this background, and with the fragrance of success in the Birmingham air, the quest for civil rights spread across the South. And whatever his doubts, King had at least found an important ally in President Kennedy who, in reiterating the principle that all men are created equal, emphasised the point that 'the rights of every man are diminished when the rights of one man are threatened'.[110]

The dream and the reality

The summer of 1963 was a simmering one. Marches and confrontations amounted to what King described as a *great shout for freedom* which echoed from coast to coast, a sharp shock which awakened millions of white-Americans from their ethical and moral slumber to reconsider the real social abuse of their times, the disadvantages of millions of fellow Americans. The country harboured two extremes – hope for millions, despair for millions – the latter being like a rising tide ever more vocal after a long, but bitter silence. The revolutionary potential of the African-American lobby had become quite real. Contrary to the sceptic's view that civil rights legislation would never be passed in Congress, King's belief that it would never wavered.

As a trade-off for his wide-ranging Bill banning segregation in public places, including hotels, theatres and shops, President Kennedy asked King to stop the demonstrations until it had been passed by Congress. King refused. He believed the longer the action continued, the greater the likelihood of getting a Civil Rights Act. Thus, King the preacher became King the political opportunist. The president (and others) interpreted his position as political blackmail, but by the end of the summer, the demonstrations were continuing with a new intensity. Sensing the mood of militancy among other black leaders, one of their younger members, James Bevel suggested a massive March on Washington.[111] Projecting the protest to national level was a positive move, which King was more than willing to exploit.

To some extent, this was a direct response to the rise of the Nation of Islam, whose followers inflamed the feelings of many white Americans. For King, the NOI's emergence contributed to the divisiveness within the black community. He said he felt he was caught between two opposing forces. On the one hand, there was the force of complacency, comprising those who having lost their self-respect, had adjusted to segregation and had become insensitive to the problem and, on the other, there was the force of bitterness and hatred which came dangerously *close to advocating violence*, notably black nationalist groups such as Elijah Muhammad's Muslim movement. King said he stood between these two forces. He felt that such fears as white Americans had were likely to bring them closer to an understanding of his position in the civil rights campaign. Therefore, an escalation of his non-violent direct-action was the way forward.

At the same time, King made much of the word 'agape' as an integral part of the movement. He defined it as 'affectionate love or friendship,' expressive of goodwill to all men and ultimately a 'willingness to die on the cross' so that others may live.'[112]

This combination of militancy and moderation was King's strategic 'middle way,' which exposed him to criticism from the younger cadre of CORE, SNCC and Black Power activists such as Stokely Carmichael, Rap Brown, Huey P Newton, James Farmer, James Forman and John Lewis, among others. So, arising from the greatest good for the greatest number, King hoped for a coalition of interests across the social spectrum in order to gain the optimum political clout.[113]

I have a dream

If Washington was, as King said, a *city of spectacles*, what it was about to witness could not be predicted. On 28 August, the capital was the scene of a huge assembly of people, the grandest that had ever come together. An estimated 250,000 came from every

King addresses crowds gathered at the Prayer Pilgrimage

part of the nation. Among them were top leaders and famous personalities, but the stunning feature of this mammoth gathering was King's base, the masses of ordinary people imbued with an unbending will to bring about democracy in their lifetime.

King observed other features of this overwhelming togetherness. Unlike Birmingham, here in Washington, there was the strong presence of representatives from white churches. He noted the absence of anger or bitterness, but this did not mean a lack of strength and dignity. Clearly, the passion for justice and freedom animated the vast crowd. The buzz among them was good-natured, but unmistakeably purposeful. Ahead of them was the edifice of Government and everyone gazed straight at it.

King had made countless speeches and spoken the word of God from many pulpits. Now, unlike anything he had done before, he was called upon to address the multitude. The responsibility of addressing the nation was huge. What sort of presentation would the preacher King deliver? How did he prepare for this?

His speech was put together hastily, parts of it in New York and others in Washington. The night before delivering it, he had arrived in the capital at about 10pm, booked into a hotel and worked on it until 4am.

With the imposing image of Abraham Lincoln as the backdrop, King approached the microphone and began to read the prepared text.

I am happy to join you today in what will go down in history as the greatest demonstration for freedom in the history of our nation. Five score years ago, a great American, in whose symbolic shadow we stand today signed the Emancipation Proclamation. This momentous decree came as a great beacon light of hope to millions of Negro slaves, who had been seared in the flames of withering injustice. It came as a joyous daybreak to end the long night of their captivity.

Coloured, textured by his unique cadence and style, these words reached receptive ears that were now sensitised to recognising the rareness of the moment. King reminded the audience:

But one hundred years later, the Negro is still not free...And so we've come here today to dramatize a shameful condition....

The strength of his conviction and clarity of thought demanded attention. With the articulation and intonation of a speaker guided by a script, he reached a point where he stopped reading. It was as though he had felt the pulse of the audience pull him farther and farther away from the prepared text. Without breaking his rhythm, he gazed over the podium and microphones and spoke from memory. Now, a phrase he had used before, 'I Have A Dream', came to him suddenly and like a revelation these words accumulated power with repetition. He allowed his instinct to dictate the flow of words.

If compared with his other speeches, 'I Have a Dream' lacked the sheer force of his oratory in the more intimate settings of church services and mass meetings, no one can deny its content and timely delivery, an enriching combination that has elevated it

I HAD A DREAM 83

to being the most celebrated of King's public utterances. 'I Have A Dream' evoked all that King stood for, notably the greater assertiveness among African-Americans to stand up for their rights and the promise of revolt. But, he was also careful to articulate his 'dream' of reconciliation and racial harmony. He then articulated the 'Dream' with an eloquence unique in its time and place.

I say to you today, my friends, so even though we face the difficulties of today and tomorrow, I still have a dream. I have a dream that one day this nation will rise up and live out the true meaning of its creed, 'we hold these truths to be self-evident, that all men are created equal'. I have a dream that one day on the red hills of Georgia, sons of former slaves and sons of former slave holders will be able to sit-down together at the table of brotherhood. I have a dream that one day in the state of Mississippi, a state sweltering with heat and injustice, sweltering in the heat of oppression, will be transformed into an oasis of freedom and justice. I have a dream that my four little children will one day live in a nation where they will not be judged by the colour of their skin, but by the content of their character. I have a dream today! I have a dream that one day down in Alabama... little black boys will be able to join hands little white boys and white girls as sisters and brothers. I have a dream today![114]

King framed this vision entirely within the hallowed symbols of Americanism: the Bible, the Declaration of Independence, the Constitution, the Emancipation Proclamation and the American dream. The refrain of the patriotic song *My Country 'Tis of Thee* led to his peroration *From every mountainside let freedom ring*. Applause interceded here and there, and with each well-phrased passage, King's voice rose to a higher register to maintain its audibility. *And when this happens and when we allow freedom to ring*, he added, *when we let it ring from every village and every hamlet, from every state and every city, we will be able to speed up that day when all God's children, black men and white men, Jews and Gentiles, Protestants and Catholics, will be able to join hands and sing in the words of the old*

Negro Spiritual: 'Free at last. Free at last. Thank God almighty, we are free at last!'

King stepped back from the microphone. Thunderous applause swept over him. Americans, black and white, including Southern whites, were in awe of his performance. As spokesman for the Civil Rights Movement, he had delivered an address that was inspiring, spell-binding, a speech of such moral power that it touched millions. It was a defining moment in the history of the United States.[115]

The speech had gone beyond King's wildest dreams. It had the specialness of having moved people from all walks of life. It had become the benchmark by which all previous and subsequent civil rights utterances would be judged.

King was euphoric. He recognised that his speech was well-received. After a television interview he went home pleased. Still, he had no illusions about the struggle ahead. He knew well the gap between the 'dream' and pressing realities. But with his faith renewed, the mission now, as he said that afternoon, was to *go back to the South*.[116]

King at the Freedom March 1963

September was filled with tension. The violence against African-Americans was unrelenting and King's 'dream' was far from becoming reality. Four young black girls were bombed while at Sunday school at the Birmingham Sixteenth Street Baptist Church. This tragedy moved President Kennedy to meet King and other civil rights leaders.

This loss of young lives had a profound effect on King. The glorious promise of their childhood ended, but their deaths became symbolic of the cause. He saw them as martyrs.

What surprised and disturbed him was the lack of respect shown by the local white people, especially officials in Birmingham who chose to stay away from the children's funeral. In his eulogy of the four girls, King said: *A little child shall lead them.* He was mindful of his own children and his absence from home. But even in the midst of the sorrow and suffering borne by the bereaved families and the black community, King was able to shuttle between his private and public selves, steadfast in his praise of belief in his Maker for it was through him that he was able to find meaning in his and other people's suffering.

In the days that followed, King's thoughts were on the White House, on the exercise of executive power to put right many grievous wrongs. He was hopeful and kept his dream alive. He recalled his meeting with the president during which he worried about the possibility of civil disorder, and put his position diplomatically by explaining that for leaders like him who preached the non-violent message, if some positive action was not taken soon, the rising tensions had the potential to descend into the *worst race riot* ever seen in America.

But for all his optimism, King was only human. He did not hesitate to point out how naïve he was to expect too much from the White House. He had no illusions about a certain lack of understanding that cascaded from the White House down to the real depth and determination of the Civil Rights Movement. If there were good reasons why this was so, it was a pity and a great error on the part of the White House for African-Americans were, as King knew, as determined as ever to be free and would use the non-violent method to win their freedom.[117] Nonetheless, King could hardly deny President Kennedy's courageous stand on Civil Rights.

In the weeks after King had met Kennedy and had attended the funeral of the children, the tension was obvious. Then on

22 November gunfire rang out in Dallas, Texas. President Kennedy had been assassinated and his vice-president, Lyndon Johnson was elevated to the presidency. So soon after the school girls were bombed out of existence, the assassination of the president raised serious questions about the violent nature of American society. King was quick to comment on the failure of society to apprehend its assassins, especially when the victims of such crimes were black. It was, he said, a plague that had been spreading. He spoke of Kennedy's death and reflected upon his life as a man whom he had met and, to some extent, admired. He recognised the president's flair for leadership, his grasp of the dynamics of social change and his strong advocacy of peace. If Kennedy was unafraid of change, he was a symbol of hope, which helped to explain the grief expressed by millions.

Juxtaposed with King's magnanimity was the question: Who killed Kennedy? In the nation's soul-searching, King believed that the president was killed by a *morally inclement climate* so restrictive and intolerant that disagreement could only be expressed through violence and murder.

King also believed the death of the president revealed profound, challenging truths that should move Americans to rid the nation of segregation and discrimination. The assassination marked not only a man's death, but also reflected a *complex of illusions* which destroyed the lie that hate and violence will be directed against just a few.[118]

Protest, the 'Prize' and Malcolm X

St. Augustine

In early 1964, the SCLC and King devoted their attention to St Augustine, Florida, the oldest of American cities and a stronghold of the Ku Klux Klan. Not surprisingly, organisers of this far-right group had congregated in the St. Augustine Slave Market Plaza from various parts of the South. Few local officials were brave enough to confront the Klansmen, which did little to help Florida's anti-segregation image as a popular tourist attraction. Indeed, the Klan's action of threatening telephone calls, abusive letters, lynchings and other violent attacks, ensured the preservation of the status quo.

King arrived in St Augustine at the request of local representatives who were seeking a bi-racial committee. The fact that St Augustine was mired in hatred, violence and ignorance which seeped into the business and political life of Florida had also come to the attention of the White House. With little help or understanding from the police, the violence against black people was unprecedented and prolonged. Although hundreds of civil rights campaigners were battered and bruised during the tension-filled months by members of the KKK, King was upbeat, his optimism founded, in part, upon the encouraging deliberations on the Civil Rights Bill.

King maintained contact with state and federal officials, keeping them updated on St. Augustine's racial problems. Eventually a bi-racial committee was formed and the movement decided to halt demonstrations.

King regarded this expression of good faith as one step along the difficult, but necessary road to freedom and justice. More than this, he noted that there were signs that businessmen would comply with the civil rights movement.

Finally, when the Civil Rights Act was passed, King hailed it as a *monumental achievement* which gave true meaning to the weighty words *All men are created equal*. At this moment of joy, he was mindful of the architect, the chief promoter of the legislation – President Kennedy. Ironically, it was in the wake of his death that victory followed. Elated, King did not hide his feelings. He described the passage of the Bill as hopeful, the beginning of a second emancipation proclamation that would provide cover for equal opportunity. But he felt that this legislation was a time for re-dedication rather than celebration. He knew well that the bill would not have been tabled had it not been for the 'Negro revolt of 1963,' epitomized in Birmingham's fire hoses and the police dogs that were let loose against the courageous people who opposed such violence[119] and, to a series of events during which many were battered and martyred in the battle to desegregate the South.

King felt fortunate to have met Lyndon Johnson, but he was not awed by him. At the time, Johnson was still vice-president and while he and King did not always agree, King thought he had a good understanding of poverty and unemployment among African-Americans. But while King did not underestimate the differences between them, particularly in relation

Lyndon Baines Johnson (1908–73) was the 36th President of the US. After being elected as vice-president in 1960 under John F Kennedy, he became commander-in-chief with the latter's assassination in 1963. In 1964, LBJ won passage of the Civil Rights Act and, later, introduced his Great Society program of social welfare and civil rights legislation. As the country became further mired in Vietnam, he retired from politics in early 1968.

to the pace and tactics to be employed in dealing with the crisis, he felt Johnson's approach was sincere, realistic and, thus far, wise. And when President Johnson formally signed the Civil Rights Act in the White House on 2 July 1964 (the Act was passed on 20 June) King was standing nearby, the closest witness to a truly momentous event in American history. After he had signed the Act, President Johnson gave the pen to King.

King saw the Act as a major step in the right direction. It convinced him of the importance of demonstrations which, he said, had the potential of generating further legislative measures. He had come to realise that the federal government was more amenable to taking action when conflict had reached a point of 'crisis.' But he also recognised the creative impact of demonstrations on the social and psychological climate, which legislation could not match. The positive effects on persons who had been subjected to humiliation was undeniable for through such action African-Americans learned that unity and militancy were more constructive and more effective than bullets.

Overall, King recognised the importance of the combined forces of white and African-Americans that put it on the statute book. But, he pointed out, the Act was essentially an achievement led by African-Americans that was first written in the streets.

While the Act created a heightened awareness of ongoing economic deprivation among African-Americans, leaders of the movement realised it meant little or nothing if they could not now take the campaign a step further by adding the right of African-Americans to participate in the democratic process. Securing voting rights was crucial to realising the true meaning of citizenship.[120]

By the summer of 1964, the words 'civil rights' had become well-known across America. And not surprisingly, an increasing number of white volunteers had come to join the struggle in Mississippi. Here, during the Mississippi Freedom Summer, they participated with African-Americans campaigning for the vote.

Before King had arrived in Mississippi in July 1964, he had some weeks earlier declared that the Republican Senator Barry Goldwater's nomination for the presidency would aid racists. Why? Because King believed Goldwater expressed a philosophy that was inimical to African-American aspirations.

To add to the tension, three civil rights workers were murdered. Interestingly, Goldwater's nomination and the deaths resulted in riots not only in the South, but also in Northern cities. It was this surge forward that King dubbed the *Negro revolution* which had now gained a relentless momentum. Although he was against publicly giving his support to any Presidential candidate, the possibility of Goldwater becoming president led King to take a stand against him. King's opposition to such a man was predictable and proper. He had to be vigilant. Thus, the spectre of racism in public life and its consequences continued to trouble black Americans. But, to their credit, they had come too far to do anything less than stand firm and counteract evil.

As one young black protester in Mississippi who had confronted the local police chief declared: in the 'Negro revolution' all those African-Americans who feared white people had migrated to the north and that he, as a law-abiding officer, should realise that he had 'got to do right by the rest of us'.[121]

It was the call of freedom that had emboldened the *new Negro*, as King described his fellow campaigners, who were confident that no amount of intimidation could stop their progress. After the months and years of their long campaign, King was able to say that black Mississippians had learned the hard way and remarkably they had found an effective way of dealing with their state-wide problems. He identified recent church burnings, harassment and murders in Mississippi as directly related to African-Americans being denied the vote. Only their participation could bring about the election of worthy candidates to protect their rights

Changing the political structure in the South was a huge task, but King was inspired. He was buoyed by the courage of his maturing conviction, when undertook a tour of Mississippi as a representative of the Mississippi Freedom Democratic Party (MFDP), which was affiliated to the National Democratic Party. The people he met were *great*. They had been through hellish times and survived.

King's advocacy of Civil Rights was however, overshadowed by a plot to kill him. He had been advised not to go to Mississippi but he argued he had no choice. He had to get on with his work. To be constrained by persistent thoughts of death would nullify his efforts as the bold, fearless leader he was expected to be.

In Mississippi, he stopped at Jackson, Vicksburg and Meridian and preached freedom. His pride was evident, especially when he was with the *workers* with whom he identified, a feeling consistent with his earlier concern for the impoverished masses.

As the Conventions for the national parties approached, King saw the urgent need for a national party free of racism. Towards this end, he testified at the Democratic Convention and began by telling the delegates and the nation about the police state in which the black people of Mississippi were living. Politically, Americans of colour, should learn the lesson.

King's voice resounded as he appealed to the delegates. He emphasized the urgency and morality of his appeal and argued for the African-Americans right to vote, to be represented in the social, economic and political institutions of their own country. Disenfranchisement did not sit well in a democracy. Eventually, the convention voted to abolish seating a delegation that was racially segregated, a message which King felt would be tested by the number of blacks in northern cities registering and, eventually, voting.

When the Republican Party met in San Francisco, the far right of the party held sway. King's deep concern was, however, tempered by progress made by a coalition of labour, civil rights and intellectual and religious leaders. He felt that President Johnson should not miss the opportunity of introducing radical reforms to end the domination by racists and reactionaries of the Democratic Party's Southern power structure. Until this was achieved, the dearth of imagination and creativity in federal government thinking demanded greater effort on the part of civil rights campaigners, in particular, those who subscribed to non-violent direct action. Far from being won, he believed the battle had only begun with African-Americans still shouldering the main burden.[122]

By now, King had become a speaker in great demand, easily the most eloquent of the civil rights leaders.

Nobel Peace Prize

Towards the end of the year, King's preoccupation with the harsh political realities of life in the South proved to be exhausting. Taking no chances, he went to hospital for a general check up. On the morning after he had been admitted, he received a call informing him that he had been awarded the Nobel Peace Prize. Although he had known of his nomination, he was stunned. The heavy civil rights responsibilities he carried had blocked out all else and now, amidst the antiseptic smell and quiet of the hospital room, the news came as in a dream. Soon he was able to apply perspective to the honour, acknowledging that he was but one of many players on the stage of history. His levity engendered magnanimity. The prize, he said, was testimony to the Civil Rights Movement, a cast of hundreds of thousands who played their roles with distinction. These men, women and children constituted a 'noble' people, who were the true winners of the Nobel Prize.

Around the world, people who had never heard of King now listened. Invitations for him to visit and speak poured in. When he stopped off in London en route to Norway, he discussed *racial matters* with British politicians. He also spoke to members of the

King at a press conference at the Savoy Hotel in London in 1964

black middle class in England, who subsequently formed the Campaign Against Racial Discrimination (CARD) to fight racial injustice in Britain.[123]

While in London, King preached his famous sermon 'Three Dimensions of A Complete Life' in St Paul's Cathedral. For King and his distinguished audience, this was a treasured engagement, all the more memorable to King because of the glorious groundswell of anticipation as he made his way to receive the award and plaudits of the Swedish Academy and the world.

In his acceptance speech, King spoke of America and the future of mankind. In spite of the harsh reality of brute force, he hoped for a *brighter tomorrow*. He felt inspired and renewed his dedication to his cause. Thus, he accepted the Nobel Peace Prize with *an abiding faith in America and an audacious faith in mankind*.[124] To achieve these ends, he insisted that the non-violent method was crucial in answering contemporary political and moral questions. In overcoming oppression and violence, provocation was not an option.[125]

After these words, he turned to those closest to him. He thanked his supporters and his family, reserving the greatest praise for Coretta to whom he owed his *biggest debt*, the person who gave his life *meaning*.

After his ceremonial speech, with his new status and in the glare of unprecedented publicity, King strode the international stage. In a lecture at the University of Oslo, he spoke like a statesman, pleading with the rich nations to take positive measures to narrow the gap that separated a rich minority and the poor masses.

Ironically, while King was an honoured guest in many European countries, the contemporary racial, social and political perceptions and attitudes in America were reflected in the treatment he received from US ambassadors who ignored him in Europe.[126] Nonetheless, the award solidly confirmed his position

Martin Luther King Jr with Coretta Scott King

as a prophet, whose humanitarian message of resisting violence struck warm responses among people around the world.

For the Atlanta-born preacher, 1964 was a highly unusual year. Almost three-quarters of the way through it, King visited West Berlin at the invitation of Mayor Willy Brandt. King then went to meet Pope Paul VI at the Vatican. And so after being named 'Man of the Year' by *Time* magazine at the beginning of 1964, by the end of the year, he had become the Nobel Peace Prize winner. He was thirty-five years old.[127]

On his return to America, there were calls to the SCLC to establish a footing in Northern cities. In truth, whether or not he liked it, King could no longer play only a parochial role. African-Americans beyond the South were ready to claim him and with the wider connections he had hitherto made, he was strengthened and more determined, to confront racism at home and abroad.

He identified three inter-related issues which demanded his attention: racial prejudice, poverty and war around the world.

From the time of his visit to Africa to receiving the Nobel Prize, King broadened his SCLC remit. He became more and more interested in the problems facing mankind as a whole. International issues gave perspective to local issues and vice-versa, none of which could be separated or isolated. All were integral parts of a divine pattern which he described as being *interwoven into a single garment of men's destiny.* But from such grandiloquence and light, there were indications of darker moments. He was, at times, disheartened by an age which was heading to its doom. Rarely had he felt as gloomy as now and not surprisingly he invoked the hope of a 'new direction.'

So, in spite of his elevation to the mountaintop, King felt the need to return to the valley. He said something told him that the true test of a man is not when times were good, or when things were in his favour, but when he was confronted with challenge and upheaval.[128] He had been sensitive to the rumblings for some time and knew there was no dearth of controversy to come. As it was, attempts by the FBI to discredit him – especially over his infidelities – persisted.

Malcolm X

The harassment of Malcolm Little's father by the Ku Klux Klan and the mistreatment of his mother who had suffered a mental breakdown was cause enough for a deprived boy to become bitter. But in spite of this, young Malcolm had ambition, which unfortunately led him to dead-end jobs, then to selling and using drugs and to burglary which landed him in prison. Here, he was introduced to the Nation of Islam which had originated in the early years of the Great Depression and grew steadily. On his release from prison in 1952, Malcolm joined the black Muslims and became a recruiter. Soon he changed his name to 'X' rather than carry his slave name. He rose steadily through the NOI's ranks and became one of the most outspoken and popular black

Muslims. Among blacks involved in the emerging Civil Rights Movement, he could be counted among the most extreme in his views. There were basic differences between Malcolm's position and that of the NAACP, CORE and SCLC leaders. He believed that racial equality and integration could not be achieved and that it was foolish to think that the strategy of non-violent confrontation could bring about equal rights. He maintained his outspokenness and by 1961 he was already being criticised by the NOI's leadership and soon there was open disagreement as he reassessed his position in NOI. But by then and even moreso, four years later, his contribution to civil rights was secure: he had transformed the consciousness of a generation of African-Americans from self-hatred to racial pride which was crucial to the struggle for equality.

King's respect for Malcolm X was not boundless. There were limits, the most obvious being Malcolm's advocacy of violence which King strongly opposed. But King conceded Malcolm's eloquence in expressing his views and commitment to the problems of African-Americans. Beyond adversarial respect, King also had a *deep affection* for Malcolm, although they did not know each other as friends.

On 26 March 1964, King and Malcolm met briefly after a Press conference; and when King was pelted with eggs in New York, he blamed Malcolm's black nationalists. He said these supporters of Malcolm had heard he was malleable and talked a good deal about love and that much of the anger and bitterness they felt toward the white man was directed to him. King dismissed thoughts about himself as an 'Uncle Tom' and felt aggrieved that he was misunderstood by the Black Power advocates. Nonetheless, he saw Malcolm as a 'victim of despair' because he, like so many African-Americans, felt a sense of 'nobodyness' which the system of racial injustice had created.

Overall, King was not lacking in empathy or sympathy for Malcolm. Given his depth of understanding, he reflected upon

Malcolm's articulation of the 'Hate That Hate Produced,' hate that had arisen because, he grew up in an environment that was hopeless, that lacked sympathetic preachers, teachers and a grounding in the importance of non-violence to the black struggle. But King also recognised Malcolm's natural talents: his innate intelligence, energy and ambition which so clearly needed to be channelled and expressed. He had depth and integrity, King observed, but sadly while Malcolm was still striving for fulfilment, he was brutally cut down.

It needs to be said that left to King, Malcolm would never have been invited to Selma, simply because of their antithetical philosophies. Be that as it may, while King was locked up in a Selma jail, Malcolm visited Coretta. According to King, Malcolm had a long talk with Coretta, during which he had indicated a desire to collaborate with the non-violent movement. He also showed an interest in adopting political means to deal with the black community's problems.

To King, the lesson to be learnt from the assassination of Malcolm X in 1965 was that violence and hate did not stem the flow but incited more of both. He insisted that brotherhood and love were crucial to the leadership of the African-American people. Anything less would be self-destructive. Stokely Carmichael disagreed. In a sense, Malcolm's life and death could not be more illustrative of King's views, all the more because this tragedy coincided with Malcolm's re-evaluation of his Black Power position vis-à-vis the non-violent movement and a less generalised attitude to white people. The narrow, sectional approach to the black struggle as a way out of the dilemma of racial discrimination was, to King's mind, barmy. The replacement of one form of tyranny by another would solve nothing. Instead, African-Americans should not seek a position of advantage, but should seek fairness through the creation of a moral environment from which brotherhood and democracy could arise.[129]

To most black Americans, including Black Power militants, such reasonable statements by King were far-off the mark. They were, as a consequence, interpreted as too idealistic, especially in the face of police violence and brutality in the South.

SCLC campaigns and black power

Selma

In 1965, the right to vote continued to preoccupy King. He recalled his meeting with President Johnson the previous year. On his way back from Scandinavia, King had stopped to see the president who agreed with him on getting a Voting Rights Bill through, but he stressed that it all came down to timing. He would do it eventually, the president declared, but for the moment, there were other Bills on his agenda which would help African-Americans. King's response was to the point: political reform was fundamental to all the relevant problems. Johnson replied that he would not alienate his white supporters in the South because their votes were necessary if he was to get the Voting Rights Bill passed by Congress. As their talk ended in stalemate, King urged the president to do his *best*.

King's next move could not have been clearer. And so it was that within a mere two weeks of his return he moved to Selma, Alabama.

In this town, white people were the majority, representing 99 per cent of the population. Here, as in the adjoining counties, African-Americans were denied the vote. Here, aggressive white racists saw outspoken black men and women as legitimate targets. Put simply, Selma was no less oppressive a place for African-Americans than many other parts of the South.

In a statement to the press, King outlined the difficulties that African-Americans faced in their attempts to register in Selma and Dallas County. To counteract the ridiculous barriers to registration, the intention was to wage a relentless war on malpractices until democracy was established.

Unsurprisingly, after the Voting Rights March in Selma early in February 1965, King was arrested and jailed. When he was freed four days later, he flew to see Vice-President Hubert Humphrey. At their meeting, King pressed the case for all citizens to exercise the right to vote without harassment, intimidation, police violence and without delay. Frustration among African-Americans had grown markedly, and he underlined the fact that more black people were in Selma jails than there were black people on the voting register. Clearly the slow progress was calculated to maintain the political power structure in the South. Before he left, King requested that an injunction be brought against the prosecution of thousands of African-Americans in Selma and again, he urged passage of voting rights legislation.[130]

Against this background, the scene was set for confrontation on the proposed March from Selma to Montgomery. Once more, the strategy was the use of non-violence to dramatise the existence of injustice and, therefore, reinforce the quest for justice. King was aware of the concern of those closest to him about his personal safety. Death threats and an attempt to assassinate him had implications on his appearance as leader of the March. He had turned over this possibility in his mind many times and, regardless of the risk, he felt that his conscience must be his guide.

But for all its inherent worry, this was not King's only preoccupation. It was his duty as pastor to serve his parishioners first before leading the March from Selma.

Governor Wallace's ban on the march alerted King of the possibility that state troopers would arrest all those who participated. But King was unprepared for the brutality of the troopers. Violent repression was followed by frantic deliberations on the part of King and his SCLC associates, including consultation with his lawyers as to the course of action to be taken. The route was

A military policeman keeps pace with the march to Selma led by Martin Luther King Jr

set and King headed the March until it was stopped by troopers on Highway 80. What the marchers uncovered here was the *presence* of violence as they queried the legality of their march. Once this was established, the likelihood of a bloody confrontation diminished and King led the marchers back to the safety of the Church. But on 11 March, he received information that the Unitarian minister Rev James Reeb who was in Selma had been beaten to death by the police.

If President Kennedy was moved to act by the threatening crisis in Birmingham, President Johnson expressed his outrage at the events in Selma. He surprised many people by calling upon Congress to consider a Voting Rights Bill as soon as possible. His demand was so uncompromising and his speech so passionate, that one activist John Lewis described it as perhaps the 'strongest speech any American President has ever made on the subject of Civil Rights.'[131] In part, President Johnson said: 'At times, history and fate meet at a single time in a single place to shape a turning point in man's unending search for freedom. So it was at Lexington and Concord. So it was a century ago at Appomattox. So it was last week in Selma, Alabama.'[132]

The speech was all the more important because Johnson, a Texan, was a Southerner. 'Their cause must be our cause too,' he said in conclusion, 'because it's not just Negroes, but really it's all of us, who must overcome the crippling legacy of bigotry and injustice.'

The president ended his address with the words: 'And we shall overcome.'[133]

After the march was stopped and the legal and constitutional rights were cleared, more and more people from the various states of America poured into Selma to support the campaign. King was encouraged enough to predict that the march would be of the same importance in American history as Gandhi's march to the sea was in Indian history. Such an undertaking warranted detailed planning. As a figure-head, King was seen as the architect of the march and, as such, he was able to secure the trust of many white men and women marchers. Here and there, whites gave lifts to black hitch-hikers which, at the time, was a risky thing to do especially in that part of the South.[134]

As it turned out, the Selma to Montgomery march did not disappoint its participants. It was, as Richard Deats put it, 'a fervent, holy pilgrimage, an expression of the faith of a people who would not turn back'. Rabbi Abraham Heschel likened the marchers to the Israelites and regarded them as giving their total commitment to the cause of freedom.

On the last night on the road, the marchers stopped at St Jude, a Catholic stronghold. Over 20,000 people had gathered that evening for a four-hour outdoor concert organised by Harry Belafonte. Among the entertainers present were Sammy Davis, Jr, Dick Gregory, Leonard Bernstein, Joan Baez, Tony Bennett, Peter, Paul and Mary, Ossie Davis and Odetta.[135]

As the March approached Montgomery, the United States

Justice Department warned that there was a sniper in the outskirts of Montgomery waiting to assassinate King and advised that he should drop out. King not only refused, but continued to walk at the front of the March.

The long march took its toll on the thousands who braved it. Footsore and weary, nearing the end of their 54-mile trek, they saw the great dome of the State Capitol of Montgomery, the cradle of the Confederacy. It was an uplifting sight that generated great optimism among the 50,000 marchers who crowded round that warm spring afternoon to serve notice, through petition, to Governor George Wallace.[136]

To the exhausted but elated gathering, King said it was his conviction that segregation in Alabama was dying. Of this he had no doubt. The uncertainty was really to do with the cost of the funeral which was entirely a matter for the segregationists. He reminded the crowd that the right to exercise the vote was central to the campaign in Alabama. The aim of the March was, therefore, to highlight the denial of this and to expose the well-spring of Southern segregation. Thus far, the distance the civil rights movement had travelled pointed to future moves and he warned that the momentum must be maintained even though the road ahead was a difficult one.

Importantly, King emphasized that the defeat or humiliation of the white man must, at all costs, be avoided for the aim was to gain his trust, his friendship and understanding. To the question: how long will it take? *Not long*, he answered, *because mine eyes have seen the glory of the coming of the Lord*, and, on the journey to come truth will be his followers' guide and companion. They represented one of the *most magnificent expressions of the ecumenical movement that I have ever seen*. The coming together of protestants, catholics and Jews beautifully dramatised the injustices and indignities of African-Americans in Alabama and all across the South on the fundamental question of the right to vote.

For the church, the Selma March had not only brought about the 'second great awakening' but also gave renewed vitality and meaning to the gospel. How unlike the situation that had created his 'Letter' in Birmingham this was.

Support also came from the labour movement and intellectuals. Some 40 of America's top historians had joined the March, at the end of which the cross-section of American society that had gathered mingled with rare comradeship, a semblance of the genuine brotherhood that King had hoped to see.

Alas, the climax of this great and successful campaign was followed by 'wanton and senseless' violence as the marchers in various ways headed back to Selma, some getting lifts from friendly whites such as Ms Viola Liuzzo, a white woman from Detroit, a marcher who was moved by what she had seen on television. Driving with a young black man, her car was attacked and she was shot dead. Her passenger's life was spared only because he pretended to be dead.[137]

Although King could not be sure, there was no denying that President Johnson's initiatives were honourable. After making his passionate plea for human rights before Congress, this president had made good his promise. The Voting Rights Act was passed on 6 August 1965 just a few months after the Selma to Montgomery March. The President's signature laid the basis for a 'sea change' in Southern politics, as more African-Americans were elected. This shifted the imbalance and white candidates were now confronted with the real issues affecting black people.[138]

So the brutal forces arraigned against African-Americans in Selma led to confrontations that magnified local problems, thus adding to civil rights issues at the national level. Their claims could no longer be ignored. At last, the Voting Rights Act of 1965, described by President Johnson as 'one of the most monumental laws' in the history of American freedom, was enacted.

Watts and Chicago

Soon after smouldering hatred in the South had been exposed, ferocious riots exploded in the north. Watts in Los Angeles was the location and focus of tensions and potential violence. By mid-August 1965, racial violence had claimed over 30 lives. King was warned not to go there, but he did. He walked through the devastated business district of Watts and spoke to those who had gathered because of core issues: jobs, housing, racism and the general despair of black people in ghettoes that dotted the north and west seed-beds from which the violence rose. As King argued, everyone was to blame for the *days of anguish* in Watts.

After his visit, King said that such a public display of brutality was a major issue. Riots, he stated, were angry responses from a powerless people. The release that rioters felt was almost joyous. They believed their actions were justified; they felt like 'somebody'. Clearly, their problems had to be addressed.

In all that he had said after the tragedy of Watts, King never lost sight of the economic problems: ongoing high unemployment, poverty, lack of proper medical facilities and overcrowding. But Watts was not alone in the difficulties it faced. Non-violence, King argued, was still the best approach in tackling the problems head-on. After he had discussed the impasse in Los Angeles, with President Johnson, King showed a readiness to rise to the challenge.[139]

By now, King was like a magnet, unconsciously drawing to himself all those who were engaged in the fight for equality. In the summer of 1965, black leaders in Chicago invited him to join their struggle in which education was of special interest. Sometime later, the SCLC put its full weight behind creating a strong non-violent movement in the north, citing the deprivations of African-Americans in Chicago as a 'prototype' of the northern race problem.

In an effort to knock down the wall of segregation, the Rev.

James Bevel headed an 'advance' SCLC team. His task was to lay the basis for the work of the civil rights movement. In King's view, conditions in Chicago were deplorable,[140] in particular the Lawndale slum which he described as *truly an island of poverty*. This was all the more shameful because, at the time, Chicago could boast being second to none, the highest per capita income city in the world.

King had spent some time in the city and spoke movingly of the consequences of emotional and environmental deprivation of the children's inadequate clothing. Medical neglect was unforgivable because children died needlessly. Add to this 'price fixing' and 'wholesale robbery' by many merchants and retailers, and the needs among the poorest for essential goods and services becomes increasingly desperate. Nonviolent direct-action, he maintained, was still the most effective way of challenging the status quo. After he had spoken to President Johnson about the 'deadlock' in Los Angeles, King said the President was ready to provide the statesmanship so necessary in those trying times. King was also quick to point out that aggression was born out of frustration, and to move things on, he reiterated the way forward as being through non-violent protest in the north as well. As a soldier in the field of civil rights battle, he reminded his followers (and others) of the urgency of their fight.

King understood the violence born out of the oppressive and intolerable conditions in which the slum victims lived. He spoke of his disappointment after riots in Chicago, but he was not turning his back on non-violence. Soon, in the wake of the violence, the search for scapegoats was on. The non-violent movement was seen as causing conspiracies and disaffection. Fortunately for King and his followers, these accusations did not have the desired effect. If anything, the SCLC pressed forward more firmly with its non-violent programme. Its aim now, as previously, was for a just and open society.

And so, in the summer of 1966 as the civil rights demonstrations continued in Chicago, both black and white marchers were the targets of missiles – bricks and bottles and racist obscenities. Many whites chanted 'White Power!' Though he was a seasoned campaigner, King was overwhelmed by the intensity of the hostility, the hate which surpassed all that he had seen in the South. That these racists should go to such lengths to deny individuals their legitimate rights under the American Constitution was an outrage. King regarded himself and his followers as 'social physicians,' the 'social psychiatrists' of Chicago who laid bare the malaise in the subconscious[141]. But even for such sufferers as they had identified, there was hope: he was convinced that their violent tendencies could be absorbed by the discipline of non-violence. His uncompromising belief in non-violence was, by now, clear to everyone, most of all, to the city officials who now moved closer to him and the local black leaders to expedite an agreement on housing.

Together, the Chicago and SCLC leaders, notably Jesse Jackson, took a number of initiatives in their campaign, one of which Operation Breadbasket, aimed at getting retail and consumer goods industries to reinvest profits by providing jobs within the community. King's hope was justified when in 1967 Operation Breadbasket operated in about a dozen cities.[142]

If African-Americans and Jews had a 'special' and 'unique' relationship in Chicago, it was severely tested at this time. Rent strikes and growing animosity towards Jewish landlords rankled. The black man in Chicago paid a 'Colour tax' which, King said had led to strong feelings of anti-Semitism. In the face of this, he warned against generalisation, against sloganeering. Not all Jews were exploiters of African-Americans, he insisted.

While he was keen to help the youth of Chicago, he was shocked by the degree of hatred which they harboured. Teenage boys were of particular interest. Their lives were limited, steeped in violence and degradation. Overall, his message was that non-violence and love were goals far more enriching than the violence of the slums in which they were so tragically mired. Of the boys from the South who had turned away from the path of violence, King said some of them had returned to Chicago as teachers in the service of combating evil with non-violence.[143]

Eventually, King left the 'windy city' believing that if the problems of Chicago, the nation's second largest city, could be solved, *they can be solved everywhere*. Was he being too optimistic? Or was he realistic?

When James Meredith was shot in the back in 1966, just a day or so into his Freedom March through Mississippi, King was attending a SCLC staff meeting. Early reports that Meredith was dead were, to King's relief, false and he decided to visit the wounded man. At the Municipal Hospital, Meredith expressed the hope that the marchers should continue without him. King was about to leave Meredith's bedside when Stokely Carmichael came in and

King and Stokely Carmichael together at the voter registration march 1966

extended his hand in greeting. In the brief dialogue that followed, both men agreed that they should leave Meredith to get some sleep and rest.

Later, King headed a group of marchers who travelled to the spot where Meredith was shot. Along the way, much was said and many questions were posed, including the need for an all-black march that would take a stand against negative whites. It would mean an essentially African-American march, but King was forthright in dealing with this call. He was careful, once more, to point out that because some white people were clearly racist, black marchers should not accuse all whites of this attitude and practice. As it is with life, racial understanding had to be created. Life is what you make of it, and working together erodes fear and brings greater understanding, King argued. The Freedom March, therefore, had to be inter-racial because against a foe as formidable as the one they faced, unity was the key.

In the days that followed, talk among leaders continued as the March approached Greenwood. This was SNCC territory and Carmichael did not hide his excitement when, before a huge gathering, he launched a strong attack upon justice in Mississippi. He was followed by a SNCC speaker who shouted the need for 'Black Power!' Thus, the Black Power slogan was born as part of the Civil Rights Movement.[144]

In contrast to the integrationist and non-violent strategy of King, 'Black Power' pursued a more militant strategy. Under the guidance of leaders such as Malcolm X, it asserted that African-Americans should pursue self-determination and had the right to use violence to counter violence.

King's reservations were both instinctive and deliberative. He thought that the choice of words was unfortunate and later wrote:

I pleaded with the group to abandon the Black Power slogan. It was my contention that a leader has to be concerned about problems of semantics. Each word, I said, has a denotative meaning – its explicit and recognised sense – and a connotative meaning – its suggestive sense. While the concept of Black Power might be denotatively sound, the slogan "Black Power" carried the wrong connotations. I mentioned the implications of violence that the press had already attached to the phrase.[145]

Black Power, King felt, would cause division among the marchers. There was, however, a kind of Black Power which King felt was justified: not 'black separatism' with its racist overtones, but Black Power that promoted accession to political and economic power which would lead to equality, an end to discrimination, and therefore to full citizenship. To achieve these goals, King knew well the important role that white Americans of good will had to play. They were indispensable because it was wrong to think that a violent black campaign could be won.

Given their differences, when King, Stokely Carmichael and Floyd McKissick of CORE met, King's distaste for violence led him to plead with the young radicals to disown the Black Power slogan which, he said, was sending out the wrong signals.

For Carmichael, the objective was marshalling the political and economic resources of black people to gain power. Power wins respect and black people would achieve it regardless of the cost. He cited the Jews, Irish and Italians in America as groups that had power. Why can't we, he wondered.

To achieve this, King answered that building racial pride was crucial, but this should be based on a programme, not simply a slogan. What divided them was the means not the ends. King's position remained unchanged, and the meeting ended in stalemate with Stokely and Floyd maintaining theirs.

King regarded the African-American's revolutionary position as bearing a strong resemblance to other movements. Prior to the 20th century, he declared, nearly all revolutions were underscored by hope and hate. In this sense, the hope was of high expectations of a new system that would bring freedom and justice. King identified Gandhi's Indian movement as a revolution based *on hope and love, hope and non-violence.* Similarly, he reflected, the Civil Rights Movement in America between 1956 and 1965 had also transformed hate into non-violent power. He warned the proponents of Black Power that revolution arising from despair, cannot be *sustained by despair.*

The Black Power issue had pressed King to re-examine leadership, to consider the 'genuine' leaders from those who were not. Ultimately, he felt a true leader was not a person who sought consensus, but one who moulded consensus. Such a person was not a conformist, but someone who stood out, a person of conviction, a believer in God, one who refused to hate and opposed violence.

In the dark, confused world of power and corruption, King felt there was a desperate need in America for a 'new kind' of leader.[146]

Vietnam and the poor people's campaign

The killing fields of Vietnam was taking its toll on America. It was a political hot potato but as early as August 1965, King was deeply disturbed by developments and had decided to enter the fray. The US bombing of North Vietnam had to stop. In effect, he had become a conscientious objector.

King was heartened by President Johnson's willingness to negotiate and regarded it as a window of opportunity to be exploited. He felt it was most important for Americans to ask the right questions about the war in Vietnam. Not the question why the war, but rather how to stop the blood-letting and hasten peace talks.

'Culpability and morality' were important issues too, but, he felt they should not dominate the debate because they were likely to deflect attention and cause division. King engaged in petitions and urged the president to seek peace through negotiation. As hope gave way to disappointment, King's conscience reinforced his stance. He began to speak out against the Vietnam war to the dismay of many newspapers and newspapermen, even among African-American pressmen and civil rights campaigners. He had moved into dangerous territory, an area of concern which many reactionaries felt was beyond his province.

This was not an easy time for King, and he wisely took a break in the hope of coming to terms with all that surrounded him. He thought about writing another book, but this was not compelling enough to deflect his attention away from the war. Despite the criticism, he felt he had no choice but to stand firm. He vowed not to be silent as the lives of thousands of Vietnamese children were being destroyed. Only he could speak for himself. On 4 April 1967 in an address at the Riverside Church in New York, he was forthright in his denunciation:

We have destroyed their [the Vietnamese people] *two most cherished institutions: the family and the village. We have destroyed their land and crops... We have supported the enemies of the peasants of Saigon. We have corrupted their women and children and killed their men... What do they think as we test our latest weapons on them, just as the Germans tested out new medicine and new tortures in the concentration camps of Europe.*[147]

Truth is what mattered to King, regardless of the consequences. He was determined to tell it as God had 'revealed' it to him. And so he was viewed as a high profile deserter. His conscience remained his guide. The ultimate measure of a man is not where he stands in moments of convenience, he said, but where he stands in moments of challenge, moments of great crisis and controversy. He had reached a defining moment in his life. Although he had previously said it in different ways, now in a sermon at Ebenezer delivered on 5 November 1967, he said: 'If you have never found something so dear and so precious to you that you will die for it, then you aren't fit to live'.[148]

The Poor People's Campaign

King, the clergyman, now re-stated his calling, which was to question America, a society that produced beggars and, as such, was in need of restructuring and renewal. This is what he thought about his country in 1967 when the SCLC had decided to go to Washington to highlight the economic difficulties of African-Americans and press their case upon the government.

King's disenchantment with the government led him to propose that both the black and white poor should join forces and march together. He had certainly become more critical and had widened his political and economic concerns but he was no Marxist. He noted how economically depressed black communities had become and laid the blame squarely on policy-makers, who were shifty in their interpretation of black and white unemployment. Mass unemployment in the black community, according to King, was interpreted as 'a social problem,' whereas mass unemployment among white Americans was tagged a *depression*.[149]

As planning of the Poor Peoples Campaign proceeded, by early 1968, King was involved in a gruelling round of speeches that took him from Detroit then to Los Angeles from where he had flown to Memphis. Here, race and labour relations had hit a new low and King spoke to manual workers on strike about solidarity. By their public actions, he said, they were admitting what should be obvious: that the *haves* and the *have-nots* were inescapably tied to a *single garment of destiny*. Equality will only come with struggle.

King's support of the strike in Memphis shifted its emphasis from being a labour dispute to a 'racial conflict,' as a strike support group Community on the Move for Equality was formed. Interestingly, some of King's SCLC associates and close friends were concerned about his behaviour and appearance as he rallied support for his Poor People's Campaign. He looked weary, tired and spiritually exhausted. Normally a formal, but eminently approachable public figure, now he seemed 'very lonely' and alone. According to David Garrow, King felt guilty that he could not spend more time with his children. He regretted that they were growing up in his absence, especially his youngest Bernice who was then five. But if he had earlier been keen on the prospect of another child some time after Bernice was born, that desire cooled for, as Coretta admitted, her husband had stopped talking about 'another baby'. Now, the SCLC staffers who were closest to King had become, in a sense, his 'family'.

King with his children Yolanda and Martin Luther III at the World's fair, New York. 1964

Eventually, when the Poor Peoples' Campaign march began, it was marred by violence. King was 'confused' as angry youths clashed with the police. He wanted nothing to do with such actions and felt the need to plan another March. But the negative publicity which the violence generated deepened King's worry. Internal SCLC disagreements did not help and he felt even more isolated and depressed. Often he would immediately turn to Coretta, once the 'ideal wife' but now 'part of the problem.' Their marriage was no longer what it had been (the whispers of King's extra-marital relations became louder) and, as one of King's associates put it Coretta was 'most certainly a widow long before her husband died.' Nonetheless, she maintained her dignified bearing and performed her duties as Mrs King.[150]

Buoyed by optimism, King's hopes for freedom and justice persisted with his demanding schedule of public appearances. As always, his speeches contained many references to Biblical characters whom he used to illustrate his points. Then, his thoughts would shift to deeper preoccupations. In one speech, he confessed that he had lived with death threats every day and at times he felt discouraged, especially when abuse and criticism came from within his own community. Yes, his discouragement extended so far that at times, he felt his work was in vain. But, he never allowed such feelings to depress him unduly. *In Gilead, there is a balm to make the wounded whole.* Such words, evocative of hope even without the healing music, revived his spirit, renewed his faith and resolve in building a new Memphis. He believed in that coming day *when every valley shall be exalted. Every mountain and hill will be made low. The rough places will be made plain, and the crooked places straight. And the glory of the Lord shall be revealed, and all flesh shall see it together.*[151]

Memphis farewell

The Unfinished Journey

In the early months of 1968, King was reviewing a few of the high-points of his extraordinary life. From 5 December 1955 to April 1968, the *raison d'être* of his life was the SCLC. Ella Baker was right when she said that 'the movement made Martin rather than Martin making the movement.' But it was King, more than any other leader, who 'fused the concepts of civil, economic and human rights, and so transformed the movement itself.'[152] And given that the traditions of the Baptist Church from which he sprang were at the core of his being, clearly he had moved on. He was a complex man in whom the elements were truly mixed. By the time he had reached Memphis on 3 April 1968, he seemed to have come to terms with himself. Having lived with the spectre of death each day for so long, he was filled with a strong sense of his mortality and he had no qualms about going public with his feelings. *Every now and then*, he said in one of his last sermons, he thought about what he would like someone to say at his funeral: that he had *tried to give his life serving others*, that he believed in love, justice, peace and, yes, that he was also against war and violence. By helping others, he hoped his *living would not be in vain*.

Ralph Abernathy and Andrew Young, who were very close to King at this time, noted that he was still depressed. He worried about the state of the SCLC as he did about progress made in planning the second Poor People's Campaign March. To this end, he travelled to and from Memphis, drumming-up support. His

King lies slain at the feet of Andrew Young, Ralph Abernathy and Jesse Jackson in Memphis, Tennessee 1968

friend Abernathy went to speak at the massive Mason Temple where King had just two weeks before spoken to a capacity crowd of about 14,000 people. On arrival, the disappointing turnout of some 2,000 prompted Abernathy to request King's presence at the Temple because the people wanted to hear him. King obliged and that night was a revelation. He hinted at aspects of his state of mind, of thoughts that troubled him. In particular, he recalled the time when he was only a sneeze away from death and the words of the white schoolgirl who had written to him while he was recovering from the stab wound in 1958 saying: 'I'm so happy you did not sneeze.'

After years of foreboding, at times of desperate personal anguish, he was now foretelling his death. Much as he would have liked to live a long life *it really doesn't matter now,* he said, *because I've been to the mountaintop*. It was a privilege to have been there and to have seen the promised land but, he warned, *I may not get there with you.*[153] After preaching these prophetic words to a large gathering of the faithful on the night of 3 April, he retired to his Motel room exhausted.

The next day he seemed more at ease, but it was not one of his bright days. On his journey thus far, he had met the movers and shakers of his time and, few, if any, had truly impressed him. He was just 39 years old, but looked older. Now, as evening approached, he was dressed and ready to leave the Lorraine Motel for dinner at the home of a friend and fellow preacher. He was anticipating the 'soul food.' Those who were with him on the balcony, left his side and for a brief moment, he stood alone. Then a loud, cracking sound was heard. Moments later, he lay mortally wounded by an assassin's bullet. 'Martin, Martin,' Ralph Abernathy called out to his friend, 'can you hear me?' There was no reply from the fallen King. In the confusing silence, his muteness dramatised the echo of familiar words: *Free at last. Free at last... Thank God Almighty. I'm free at last.*

King's parents Martin Luther Snr and Alberta seated with Coretta at his memorial service 1968

ASSASSINATION

He was released from the redemptive suffering endemic in the non-violent pursuit of his 'Dream.' But although the bombs continued to rain down on Vietnam, he could hardly have imagined that his 'living had not been in vain.' For as he had said of Mahatma Gandhi, now he too belonged to the ages. He was not a saint, but a man. His genius, in part, lay in his ability to translate complex arguments of his time into simple language. 'Make it plain, son, make it plain,' his proud father urged him on early in his pastoral career. He honoured this dictum and, as the maturing preacher King became the King of preachers, less concerned with the hereafter than he was with life on earth, he created his own rich mosaic of expressions that were, and are, eminently quotable. *We must accept finite disappointment,* he said, *but we must never lose infinite hope.*

It is this abiding belief in the transforming power of his vision that moved King to speak on ethical and moral issues in a voice that, at once, touched the hearts and minds of people everywhere. Then, as now, its resonance inspires other dreams.

Notes

1. Adam Fairclough, *Martin Luther King, Jr.* (London: Cardinal/Sphere Books, 1990), p.3.
2. Fairclough, p.4.
3. Lerone Bennett, Jr, *What Manner of Man: Martin Luther King, Jr.* (London: George Allen & Unwin, 1966) pp.8-9.
4. Clayborne Carson (ed), *The Autobiography of Martin Luther King, Jr.* (New York, Warner Books), pp.4-5.
5. Stephen Oates, *Let The Trumpet Sound: A Life of Martin Luther King, Jr.* (Edinburgh: Canongate Books, 1998), p.1; Fairclough, p.6
6. *Autobiography*, p.16.
7. Carson Clayborne (ed), *The Papers of Martin Luther King, Jr*, Vol. 1, pp.33-35.
8. Bennett, pp.16-19; *Autobiography*, p.1; Fairclough, pp.5-6.
9. *Autobiography*, p.6; Richard Deats, *Martin Luther King, Jr.: A Biography* (London/New York: New City Press, 1999) p.17; Oates, p.1; Fairclough, p.6.
10. Oates, p.10.
11. *Autobiography*, pp.8-10.
12. Bennett, p.25.
13. See Letter to Martin Luther King, Sr., 15 June a944, quoted in *Autobiography*, p.11.
14. Speech 'The Negro and the Constitution' quoted in the *Autobiography*, pp. 9-10.
15. *Autobiography*, p.15; Fairclough, pp.7-8.
16. Martin Luther King, Jr, *Stride To Freedom: The Montgomery Story* (New York: Harper & Row Publishers, 1958), p.91
17. *Autobiography*, p.14.
18. Carson, *Papers of Martin Luther King, Jr.*, Vol.1, pp.37-45; *Stride To Freedom*, p.91; Autobiography, p.13.
19. Fairclough, p.8.
20. Bennett, pp.26-27.
21. Oates, p. 14.
22. Fairclough, pp.8-9.
23. Fairclough, pp. 9-10.
24. *Autobiography*, pp.17-18; Oates, pp.25-26.

25. Fairclough, pp.10-11.
26. David Garrow, *Bearing the Cross: Martin Luther King, Jr., and the Southern Christian Leadership Conference* (London: Jonathan Cape, 1988) p.40.
27. Carson, *Papers of Martin Luther King, Jr.*, Vol. 1, pp.45-57; *Stride to Freedom*, pp.94-99. *Autobiography*, p.24.
28. Howard Thurman, *With Head and Heart* (New York: Harcourt Brace, 1979) p.254; Deats, p.22.
29. Garrow, pp.44-5.
30. Fairclough, pp.12-14.
31. Coretta Scott King, *My Life With Martin Luther King, Jr.* Revised Edition. (New York: Henry Holt & Co. 1993) pp.44-9.
32. Coretta King, p.89.
33. Garrow, p.47.
34. Coretta King, pp.67-68; Garrow, pp.47-8
35. Coretta King, p.69.
36. Autobiography, pp.32-3.
37. *Autobiography*, pp.44-6.
38. *Autobiography*, pp.46-7.
39. Deats, pp.21-3.
40. Quoted in Deats, p.27.
41. *Autobiography*, pp.48-9.
42. Garrow, p.51.
43. Stride To Freedom, p.70.
44. Garrow, pp.14, 16-17; Deats, pp.32-33.
45. *Autobiography*, pp.9-10; Oates, p.16.
46. *Autobiography*, p.67
47. See *Stride To Freedom*; Deats, p.33.
48. 'Statement at MIA Meeting,' 30 January 1956 quoted in *Autobiography*, p.78; Garrow, p.625; Peter Ling, *Martin Luther King, Jr.* (London: Routledge, 2002) p.1.
49. Excerpted from the Files of the Fellowship Of Reconciliation Correspondence 1955-58. Quoted in Deats, p.35.
50. Coretta King, pp.113-114; *Autobiography*, pp.77-8.
51. *Autobiography*, p.80.
52. *New York Times*, 24 February 1956.
53. *Autobiography*, p.82.
54. King, *Stride To Freedom*, pp.142-144.
55. *Autobiography*, p.89.
56. Garrow, pp.79-80; *Autobiography*, p.93.
57. *Autobiography*, p.97.
58. *Stride To Freedom*, p.101.
59. *Autobiography*, p.100.
60. Deats, p.35.

61. Fairclough, pp.27-8.
62. *Autobiography*, p.104.
63. Fairclough, p.47.
64. *Autobiography*, pp.111-114.
65. William Robert Miller, *Martin Luther King, Jr.* (New York: Weybright & Talley, 1968) p.61; Deats, p.54; *Autobiography*, p.116.
66. Quoted in the *New York Post*, 14 August, 1957.
67. *Autobiography*, pp.105-6.
68. *Autobiography*, p.108.
69. Lerone Bennett, p.80.
70. Bennett, pp.98-100; Miller, pp.68-70; Deats, pp.55-6.
71. *Autobiography*, p.118.
72. Fairclough, p.48.
73. *Autobiography*, pp.123-4.
74. Deats, pp.57-8; Bennett, pp.101, 104.
75. *Autobiography*, p.130.
76. 'I Am An Untouchable' from a Sermon at Ebenezer Church, 4 July 1965. Quoted in *Autobiography*, p.31.
77. *Autobiography*, p.134.
78. Sermon On Gandhi delivered in Montgomery on 22 March 1959. Quoted in *Autobiography*, p.132.
79. Garrow, p.15; Oates, p.501.
80. Fairclough, pp.51-55.
81. Miller, p.84; Deats, p.59.
82. Deats, p.60.
83. Ling, pp.64-5. .
84. *Autobiography*, pp.141-3.
85. Bennett, pp.118-119.
86. Bennett, p.117.
87. Letter to Coretta, 26 October 1960. Quoted in *Autobiography*.
88. Garrow, p.148.
89. Deats, p.62.
90. Garrow, pp.154-161; Deats, pp.63-4.
91. Garrow, pp.164-5.
92. *Autobiography*, pp.154-5.
93. *Autobiography*, pp.164-5.
94. Bennett, pp.129-131. .
95. Ling, pp.103, 116.
96. Bennett, pp.133-4.
97. Garrow, p.244.
98. Bennett, pp.140-141.
99. James Washington: 'Letter from Birmingham City Jail' in *Testament of Hope*, p.29; Deats, p.71.

100. *Autobiography*, pp.191-2.
101. Deats, pp.71-2.
102. *Autobiography*, pp.197, 199.
103. *Autobiography*, pp.187, 204.
104. Washington, p.302; *Autobiography*, p.203.
105. Deats, p.73; *Autobiography*, p.205.
106. *Autobiography*, pp.205-6.
107. *Autobiography*, p.208.
108. Statement at Mass Meeting, 5 May 1963; *Autobiography*, p.210.
109. *Autobiography*, pp. 210-211, 213, 217.
110. Oates, pp.244-5.
111. Fairclough, pp.82-3.
112. Fairclough, pp.84-5.
113. August Meier: 'On the Role of Martin Luther King Jr' in Eric Lincoln (ed) *Martin Luther King Jr: A Profile* (New York: Hill & Wang 1984) pp..144-156; Fairclough, pp.85-87.
114. *Autobiography*, pp.223-228; Garrow, pp.283-4.
115. Fairclough, pp.87-8; Deats, p.82.
116. Garrow, pp.285-6.
117. *Autobiography*, pp.233-5.
118. *Autobiography*, pp.238, 253-4.
119. Bennett, pp.151-2.
120. *Autobiography*, pp.243-245.
121. *Autobiography*, pp.246-8.
122. *Autobiography*, pp.250-4.
123. *Autobiography*, pp.256-258.
124. Coretta Scott King, pp.11.
125. Washington, p224; Deats, p.91.
126. Andrew Young: *An Easy Burden: The Civil Rights Movement and the Transformation of America* (New York: HarperCollins, 1996) pp.320-326.
127. Deats, pp.90-1.
128. *Autobiography*, pp.261-2, 264.
129. *Autobiography*, pp.266-9.
130. *Autobiography*, pp.275-7.
131. John Lewis: *Marching With the Wind: A Memoir of the Civil Rights Movement in America* (Durham: British Association for American Studies, 1991); Essays edited by John H. Bracey, Jr., August Meier and Elliot Rudwick: *Conflict and Competition: Studies in the Recent Black Protest Movement* (New York: Simon and Schuster, 1998), p.339; Deats, p.98.
132. Julian Williams: *Eyes on the Prize: America's Civil rights Years 1954-1965* (New York: Viking Penguin, 1987) p.278; *Autobiography*, pp.277-283; Deats, pp.98-99.
133. Williams, Ibid.

134. Deats, pp.103-4.
135. Lewis: *Marching*, p.345; Deats, pp.101-2.
136. *Autobiography*, pp.283-4.
137. Deats, p.104.
138. *Autobiography*, p.289.
139. *Autobiography*, pp.294-6.
140. *Autobiography*, pp.298-9.
141. *Autobiography*, back ed. (London: Abacus, 2000) p.306.
142. *Autobiography*, See The Chicago Campaign, pp.295-309.
143. *Autobiography*, pp.312-3.
144. Milton Viorst: *Fire in the Streets: America in the 1960s* (New York: Simon and Schuster, 1979), p.345; John White: *Martin Luther King, Jr. and the Civil Rights Movement in America* (British Association for American Studies, 1991) p.26; *Autobiography*, pp.315-316.
145. White, pp.26-7.
146. *Autobiography*, p.332.
147. Richard Lentz: *Symbols, the News Magazines and Martin Luther King* (Baton Rouge: Lousiana State University Press, 1990) p.237; White, p.27.
148. Martin Luther King, Jr.: *In My Own words: Selected and Introduced by Coretta Scott King.* (London: Hodder & Stoughton, 2002) p.24; *Autobiography*, 344.\
149. *Autobiography*, pp.346-7, 349-250.
150. Garrow, pp.602-4; 606-7.
151. *Autobiography*, pp.254-5.
152. White, p.33.
153. Garrow, pp.620-1.

Chronology

Year	Age	Life
1929		15 January: Martin Luther King Jr born in Atlanta.
1944	15	Enter Morehouse College, Atlanta.
1947	18	Becomes assistant Pastor at Ebenezer Baptist Church, Atlanta.
1948	19	25 February: Ordained to Baptist Ministry. June: Graduates from Morehouse College with Bachelor of Arts, Sociology. September: Enters Crozer Seminary in Chester, Pennsylvania.
1951	22	Graduates from Crozer Seminary with Bachelor of Divinity. Enters the Doctoral programme at Boston University School of Theology.
1953	24	18 June: Marries Coretta Scott.

Year	History	Culture
1929	Wall Street crash. Young Plan for Germany.	First Academy Awards are announced.
1944	Allies land in Normandy: Paris is liberated. Civil war in Greece.	*Lay My Burden Down* (documentary about former slaves). Adorno and Horkheimer's essay on the 'Culture Industry'.
1947	Truman Doctrine: US promises economic and military aid to countries threatened by Soviet expansion plans. India becomes independent. Chuck Yeager breaks the sounds barrier.	Tennessee Williams, *A Streetcar named Desire*. Albert Camus, *The Plague*. Anne Frank, *The Diary of Anne Frank*.
1948	Marshall plan (until 1951). Soviet blockade of Western sectors of Berlin: US and Britain organize airlift. In South Africa, Apartheid legislation passed. Gandhi is assassinated. State of Israel founded.	Brecht, *The Caucasian Chalk Circle*. Greene, *The Heart of the Matter*. Norman Mailer, *The Naked and the Dead*. Alan Paton, *Cry, the Beloved Country*. Vittorio De Sica, *Bicycle Thieves*.
1951	Anzus pact in Pacific.	J D Salinger, *The Catcher in the Rye*.
1953	Stalin dies. Mau Mau rebellion in Kenya. Eisenhower becomes US president. Korean War ends. Francis Crick and James Watson discover double helix (DNA).	Dylan Thomas, *Under Milk Wood*. Arthur Miller, *The Crucible*. Federico Fellini, *I Vitelloni*.

Year	Age	Life
1954	25	Becomes pastor of Dexter Avenue Baptist Church, Montgomery, Alabama.
1955	26	5 June: Awarded PhD from Boston University. 17 November: Yolande Denise, first child is born. December: King elected President of Montgomery Improvement Association.
1956	27	26 January: Arrested for the first time. Home is bombed. Arrested again for travelling at 30 miles per hour in a 25 miles per hour zone.
1957	28	Southern Christian Leadership Conference (SCLC) founded and King becomes first president. 23 October: Martin Luther King III is born.
1958	29	Publishes *Stride to Freedom*. In New York, stabbed at a book signing.
1959	30	Visits India and meets Prime Minister Jawaharlal Nehru.

Year	History	Culture
1954	French withdrawal from Indochina: Ho Chi Minh forms government in North Vietnam. US Supreme Court declares segregated public schools unconstitutional in Brown vs. Board of Education.	Kingsley Amis, *Lucky Jim*. J R R Tolkien, *The Lord of the Rings*. Bill Haley and the Comets, 'Rock Around the Clock'.
1955	West Germany joins NATO. Warsaw Pact formed. Rosa Parks is arrested on 1 December in Montgomery. Thereafter, the Montgomery Improvement Association is founded.	Tennessee Williams, *Cat on a Hot Tin Roof*. Vladimir Nabokov, *Lolita*.
1956	Nikita Khruschev denounces Stalin. Suez Crisis. Revolts in Poland and Hungary. Fidel Castro and Ernesto 'Che' Guevara land in Cuba. Transatlantic telephone service links US to UK. Montgomery Bus Boycott ends on 20 December.	Lerner (lyrics) and Loewe (music), *My Fair Lady*. Elvis Presley, 'Heartbreak Hotel', 'Hound Dog', 'Love Me Tender'. John Osborne, *Look Back in Anger*.
1957	President Eisenhower uses troops to enforce school desegregation. Treaty of Rome: EEC formed. USSR launches Sputnik 1. Ghana becomes independent.	The Academy excludes anyone on the Hollywood blacklist from consideration for Oscars (to 1959).
1958	Fifth French Republic; Charles De Gaulle becomes president. Great Leap Forward launched in China (until 1960). Castro leads communist revolution in Cuba.	Boris Pasternak, *Dr Zhivago*. Claude Lévi-Strauss, *Structural Anthropology*. Harold Pinter, *The Birthday Party*.
1959	In US, Alaska and Hawaii are admitted to the Union. Solomon Bandaranaike, PM of Ceylon (Sri Lanka), is assassinated.	In Detroit, Berry Gordy founds Motown Records. Buddy Holly dies in plane crash. *Ben Hur* (dir. William Wyler). Günter Grass, *The Tin Drum*

Year	Age	Life
1960	31	Become co-pastor with his father at Ebenezer Baptist Church in Atlanta.
1961	32	30 January: Third child, Dexter, is born. 16 December: Arrested in Albany, Georgia.
1962	33	In Albany, Georgia, arrested twice.
1963	34	28 March: Fourth child, Bernice is born. April-May: Leads demonstration in Birmingham, Alabama. Writes 'Letter from a Birmingham Jail'. June: Publishes *Strength to Love*. 28 August: At Lincoln Memorial, Washington. D C, delivers 'I Have A Dream' speech.
1964	35	In Florida, leads St. Augustine march. Publishes *Why We Can't Wait*. Publicly attacked by J Edgar Hoover, director of the FBI. At the Vatican, has an audience with Pope Paul VI. Awarded the Nobel Peace Prize.
1965	36	Leads Selma Campaign for voting rights which culminates with the March from Selma to Montgomery.

Year	History	Culture
1960	Vietnam War begins (until 1975). OPEC formed. Oral contraceptives marketed. 'Sit-ins' spread across the US. John F Kennedy is elected President of the United States.	Fellini, *La Dolce Vita*. Alfred Hitchcock, *Psycho*.
1961	Berlin Wall erected. Bay of Pigs invasion. Yuri Gagarin is first man in space. In the US, 'Freedom Rides' lead to desegregation of Interstate travel.	The Rolling Stones are formed. Rudolf Nureyev defects from USSR.
1962	Cuban missile crisis. Jamaica, Trinidad and Tobago, and Uganda become independent. Satellite television launched. In the US, rioting follows the Court ordered enrolment of James Meredith at the University of Mississippi. President Kennedy federalizes Mississippi troops in September to restore order.	Edward Albee, *Who's Afraid of Virginia Woolf?* David Lean, *Lawrence of Arabia*.
1963	J F Kennedy assassinated. Kenya becomes independent. Organisation of African Unity formed. Medgar Evers, NAACP leader in Jackson, Mississippi is murdered in June. Sixteenth Avenue Baptist Church is bombed killing four girls.	Betty Friedan, *The Feminine Mystique*. The Beatles, 'She Loves You'. *Cleopatra* (Richard Burton and Elizabeth Taylor).Luchino Visconti, *The Leopard*.
1964	Khruschev ousted by Leonid Brezhnev. First race relations act in Britain. Civil Rights Act in US. PLO formed. Word processor invented. In the US, Civil Rights Act passed.	Harnick (lyrics) and Bock (music) *Fiddler on the Roof*. Saul Bellow, *Herzog*. Stanley Kubrick, *Doctor Strangelove*.
1965	Military coup in Indonesia. In the US, President Johnson signs Voting Rights Act passed on 6 August. Riots in Watts, Los Angeles, 11-16 August.	Neil Simon, *The Odd Couple*.

Year	Age	Life
1966	37	Leads campaign in Chicago, Illinois. Becomes co-chairman of Clergy and Laity Concerned about Vietnam. King becomes embroiled in Black Power controversy during Mississippi March.
1967	38	Addresses the violence of the Vietnam War and publishes *Where Do We go From Here: Chaos or Community?*, last book. Denounces war and joins peace demonstrations. Announces plans for 'Poor People's Campaign'.
1968	39	In Memphis, Tennessee, leads march in support of striking garbage workers. 31 March: At the National Cathedral (Episcopal), Washington D C, delivers final Sunday sermon. 4 April: In Memphis, assassinated on balcony of the Lorraine Motel. 9 April: In Atlanta, buried.

Year	History	Culture
1966	France withdraws its troops from NATO. In the US, race riots. James Meredith shot on his 'March Against Fear' from Memphis, Tennessee to Jackson, Mississippi.	John Lennon speculates that the The Beatles are more popular than Jesus. The band gives their last concert.
1967	Six day War. First heart transplant.	The Beatles, *Sergeant Pepper's Lonely Hearts Club Band*. Gabriel García Márquez, *One Hundred Years of Solitude*. Tom Stoppard, *Rosencrantz and Guildenstern are Dead*.
1968	Tet Offensive. In US, Robert Kennedy assassinated; President Johnson announces he will not stand for re-election; Civil Rights Act of 1968, prohibiting discrimination in housing In Paris, student riots.	Kubrick, *2001: A Space Odyssey*. The Rolling Stones, *Beggar's Banquet*.

Further Reading

For works relating to the general context to many of the problems affecting African-Americans in the South and elsewhere prior to the birth of Martin Luther King, Jr and indeed in his early life, reference must be made to the following texts: Mary Beth Norton et al, *A People and A Nation: A History of the United States* (Boston: Houghton Mifflin, 1998); James and Lois Horton, *Hard Road To Freedom: The Story of African America* (New Brunswick: Rutgers University Press, 2001); Raymond Wolters, 'The New Deal and the Negro,' in John Braem, Robert H. Bremner and David Brody, eds. *The New Deal: The National Level* (Columbus: Ohio State University Press, 1975), pp.170-217; Nancy J. Weiss, *Farewell to the Party of Lincoln: Black Politics in the Age of FDR* (Princeton, New Jersey: Princeton University Press, 1983); and Howard Sitkoff, *A New Deal for Blacks: The Emergence of Civil Rights as a National Issue*, Vol. 1, *The Depression Decade* (New York: Oxford University Press, 1978).

On African-Americans and the second world war see: Neil A Wynn, *The African-American and the Second World War* (London: Paul Elek, 1976); A Russell Buchanan, *Black Americans in World War II* (Santa Barbara, California: ABC-Clio Press, 1977); Philip McGuire, *Taps for a Jim Crow Army: Letters From Black Soldiers in World War II* (Santa Barbara, California: ABC-Clio Press, 1983); and the following articles: Richard M. Dalfiume: 'The "Forgotten Years" of the Negro Revolution',

Journal of American History, 55 (1968) pp. 90-106; Clayton R Koppes and Gregory D Black: 'Blacks, Loyalty and Motion Picture Propaganda in World War II', *Journal of American History*, 73 (1986), pp.383-406; and Robert Korstad and Nelson Lichtenstein: 'Opportunities Found and Lost: Labour, Radicals and the Early civil rights movement', *Journal of American History*, 75, (1988), pp.786-811.

The march on Washington movement and its chief architect are considered in Paula A Pfeffer, *A Philip Randolph: Pioneer of the civil rights movement* (Baton Rouge: Louisiana State University Press, 1990). On the Congress of Racial Equality see: August Meier and Elliott Rudwick, CORE: *A Study in the civil rights movement, 1942-1968*.

There has been a considerable body of writing (and audio-visual presentations) on aspects of the post-second world war civil rights movement. Some also relate to Martin Luther King, Jr., and his relationship to the Southern Christian Leadership Conference (SCLC) and the civil rights coalition. Introductory works include provided by three recent review articles: George Rehin: 'Of Marshalls, Myrdals and King's, 'Some Recent Books about the Second Reconstruction', *Journal of American Studies*, 22 (1988), pp.87-103; Adam Fairclough, 'Historians and the civil rights movement', *Journal of American Studies*, 24 (1990), pp.387-398; and Steven F Lawson: *Freedom Then, Freedom Now: The Historiography of the Civil Rights Movement*, American Historical Review, 96 (1991), pp. 456-471. These can be supplemented by an interesting collection of essays edited by Charles W Eagles, *The Civil Rights Movement in America* (Jackson and London: University of Mississippi Press, 1986); but see also William H. Chafe's essay 'The Civil Rights Revolution, 1945-1960: The Gods Bring Threads to Webs Begun', in Robert H. Bremner and Gary W. Reichard, eds, *Reshaping America: Society and Institutions* (Columbus: Ohio

State University Press, 1982), pp.68-100, an extremely perceptive piece, which appears in revised form in Chafe's excellent text *The Unfinished Journey: America Since World War II*, 2nd Edition (New York and Oxford: Oxford University Press, 1991). Manning Marable, *Race, Reform and Rebellion: The Second Reconstruction in Black America, 1945-1982* (London: Macmillan Press, 1984), analyses the civil rights movement in relation to wider American domestic politics. Harvard Sitkoff's *The Struggle for Black Equality, 1954-1980* (New York: Hill and Wang, 1981), is a useful account and assessment. The complex issues of the civil rights movement are presented in Robert Weisbrot's *Freedom Bound: A History of America's Civil rights movement* (New York and London: W W Norton, 1990).

C. Vann Woodward's *The Strange Career of Jim Crow* (New York: Oxford University Press, 1974), focuses on the aims and objectives of (and the growing tensions within) the civil rights movement during the 1950s and 1960s. Howard Rabinowitz, *The First New South, 1865-1920* (Arlington Heights: Harland Davidson, 1992); Peter Daniel, *Breaking New Land: The Transformation of Cotton, Tobacco and Rice Cultures Since 1880* (Urbana: University of Illinois Press, 1985) and *Standing At the Crossroads: Southern Life in the Twentieth Century* (Baltimore: John Hopkins University Press, 1996); Numan Bartley, *The New South, 1945-1980* (Baton Rouge: Louisiana University Press, 1995.

For works on the early and later civil rights struggle see: Aldon Morris, *The Origins of the Civil Rights Movement: Black Communities Organising For Change* (New York: Free Press, 1984); Manning Marable, *Race, Reform and Rebellion* (Jackson: University Press of Mississippi, 2001); R. Weisbrot, *Freedom Bound: A History of the Civil Rights Movement* (New York: W W Norton, 1990). Steven Lawson, Running *For Freedom: Civil Rights and Black*

Politics in America Since 1941 (New York: McGraw Hill, 1997); Harvard Sitkoff, *The Struggle for Black Equality* (New York: Hill and Wang, 1993); Robert Cook, *Sweet Land of Liberty? The African-American Struggle for Civil Rights in the Twentieth Century* (London: Longman, 1998); V. Sanders, *Race Relations in the USA Since 1900* (London: Hodder & Stoughton Educational, 2000); John White, *Martin Luther King, Jr. and the Civil Rights Movement in America* (Durham: British Association for American Studies, 1991)

Essays edited by John H. Bracey, Jr, August Meier and Elliott Rudwick, *Conflict and Competition: Studies in the Recent Black Protest Movement* (Belmont, California: Wadworth Publishing, 1971). The Supreme Court's 1954 Brown decision is comprehensively dealt with in Richard Kluger's *Simple Justice: The History of Brown v Board of Education and Black America's Struggle for Equality*, 2 vols. (New York: Knopf, 1975, 1976); and by Daniel Berman, *It Is So Ordained: The Supreme Court Rules on School Segregation* (New York: W W Norton, 1966). See also Raymond Wolters, *The Burden of Brown: Thirty Years of School Desegregation* (Knoxville: University of Tennessee Press, 1984). Eisenhower's views on civil rights are discussed in Robert Frederick Burk: *The Eisenhower Administration and Black Civil Rights* (Knoxville: University of Tennessee Press, 1985); and by Michael S. Mayer, 'With Much Deliberation and Some Speed: Eisenhower and the Brown Decision,' *Journal of Southern History*, 52 (1986), pp.43-76.

The NAACP's struggle for equal educational opportunities is discussed in Mark V. Tushmet *The NAACP's Legal Strategy Against Segregated Education, 1925-1950* (Chapel Hill: University of North Carolina Press, 1987). See also Catherine A Barnes, *Journey From Jim Crow: The Desegregation of Southern Transit* (New York: Columbia University Press, 1983); Jack Bloom, *Class, Race and the Civil Rights Movement* (Bloomington:

Indiana University Press, 1987) and Doug McAdam, *Political Protest and the Development of Black Insurgency* (Chicago: University of Chicago Press, 1999);

For Southern opposition to the civil rights movement see Numan V Bartley, *The Rise of Massive Resistance: Race and Politics in the South During the 1950s* (Baton Rouge: Louisiana State University Press, 1969); and Neil R. McMillen, *The Citizens' Council: Organized Resistance to the Second Reconstruction, 1954-1964* (Urbana: University of Illinois Press, 1971). See also: David Alan Horowitz, 'White Southerners' Alienation and Civil Rights: The Response to Corporate Liberalism, 1956-1965,' *Journal of Southern History*, 54 (1988), pp.173-200. The varying responses of entrepreneurs to the Southern phase of the movement are analysed in Elizabeth Jacoway and David R. Colburn, eds., *Southern Businessmen and Desegregation* (Baton Rouge: Louisiana State University Press, 1982). See also Anthony J. Badger's review essay, 'Segregation and the Southern Business Elite,' *Journal of American Studies*, 18 (1984), pp.105-109.

David R Goldfield argues in *Black, White and Southern: Race Relations and Southern Culture 1940 to the Present* (1990) that the great achievement of the struggle was its 'restorative effect on (southern) culture'. Clayborne Carson, *In Struggle: SNCC and the Black Awakening of the 1960s* (Cambridge, Massachusetts: Harvard University Press, 1981), deals perceptively with the most 'radical' of civil rights organisations and there is useful material in an earlier study: Howard Zinn, SNCC: *The New Abolitionists* (2nd Ed., Boston: Beacon Press, 1965). Nancy J Weiss, *Whitney M. Young, Jr. and the Struggle for Civil Rights* (Princeton: Princeton University Press, 1989), is a sympathetic account of one of King's notable contemporaries and leader of the National Urban League.

The movement at the rank and file, community level has only

recently begun to be studied. Particularly recommended are: William H. Chafe, *Civilities and Civil Rights: Greensboro, North Carolina and the Black Struggle For Freedom* (1980), Robert J. Norell, *Reaping the Whirlwind: The Civil Rights Movement in Tuskegee* (1985); David R Colburn, *Racial Change and Community Crisis: St. Augustine, Florida, 1877-1980* (New York: Columbia University Press, 1985); and James W Button, *Blacks and Social Change: Impact of the Civil Rights Movement in Southern Communities* (1989), a comparative study of several Florida towns. For civil rights confrontation in the north see Alan B Anderson and George W Pickering, *Confronting the Colour Line: The Broken Promise of the Civil Rights Movement in Chicago* (1986).

Sociological studies of the civil rights movement-relating to their localized nature can be found in Doug McAdam, *Political Process and the Development of Black Insurgency, 1930-1970* (1982); and Aldon D Morris, *The Origins of the Civil Rights Movement: Black Communities Organize for Change* (1984). On the civil rights coalition see Jack M Bloom, *Class, Race and the Civil Rights Movement* (Bloomington: Indiana University Press, 1987), and Herbert H Hines *Black Radicals and the Civil Rights Mainstream* (Knoxville: University of Tennessee Press, 1988); focus on Martin Luther King, Jr. For invaluable first-hand accounts of the civil rights struggle (with frequent references to and anecdotes about King) see Sheyann Webb and Rachel West Nelson in *Selma, Lord Selma: Girlhood Memories of the Civil Rights Days as Told to Frank Sikora* (Tuscaloosa: University of Alabama Press, 1980); Howell Raines, ed. *My Soul Is Rested: Movement Days in the Deep South Remembered* (1977, 1983); David J Garrow, ed., *The Montgomery Bus Boycott and the Women Who Started It: The Memoir of Jo Ann Gibson Robinson* (1987); Cynthia Stokes Brown, ed., *Ready From Within: Septima Clark and the Civil Rights Movement* (Navarro,

California: Wild Tree Press, 1986); Alice Walker, *In Search of Our Mother's Gardens: Womanist Prose* (New York: Harcourt Brace Jovanovich, 1984); and in the two companion volumes to the award-winning television series *Eyes On the Prize, Juan Williams, ed., Eyes on the Prize: America's Civil Rights Years 1954-1965* (New York: Viking Penguin, 1987); and Henry Hampton, Steve Fayer and Sarah Flynn eds., *Voices of Freedom: An Oral History of the Civil Rights Movement from the 1950s through the 1980s* (1990).

For women in the civil rights struggle, see Vicki L Crawford, Jacqueline Rouse and Barbara Woods, eds., *Women in the Civil Rights Movement: Trailblazers and Torchbearers, 1941-1965* (New York: Carlson Publishing, 1990), an important collection of essays on the roles and problems of black women- as organisers, activists and churchgoers 'in leading and sustaining the movement in local communities throughout the South'. In her essay 'The Role of Black Women in the civil rights movement' Ann Standley shows how 'Black women directed voter registration drives, taught in freedom schools and provided food and housing for movement volunteers (and) were responsible for the movement's success in generating popular support for the movement among rural blacks.' In Standley's view, the movement gave black men and women a sense of empowerment. See also Peter Ling and S Montieth, eds., *Gender in the Civil Rights Movement* (1999)

MARTIN LUTHER KING, JR AND RELATED STUDIES

The literature on King has grown steadily, including a number of biographies: David Levering, Lewis King: *A Critical Biography* (2nd rev. ed, Urbana: University of Illinois Press, 1978) also his essay 'Martin Luther King, Jr., and the Promise of Nonviolent Populism', in John Hope Franklin and August Meier, eds., *Black Leaders and the Twentieth Century* (1982, pp.277-303); Stephen B Oates *Let the Trumpet Sound: The Life of Martin Luther King, Jr.*, (1982); see also Oates's essay 'The Intellectual Odyssey of Martin Luther King', *Massachusetts Review*, 22 (1981), pp.301-320. David J Garrow's authoritative works include: *Protest at Selma: Martin Luther King Jr. and the Voting Rights Act of 1965* (New Haven: Yale University Press, 1978), a detailed account of the SCLC campaign and its consequences, *The FBI and Martin Luther King: From "Solo" to Memphis* (New York: W W Norton, 1981) argues that King became radical in his last years, and was distrusted by the Establishment; *Bearing the Cross: Martin Luther King, Jr. and the Southern Christian Leadership Conference* (1986) and *Martin Luther King, Jr: Civil Rights Leader, Theologian and Orator; The Walking City: The Montgomery Bus Boycott 1955-56 and Birmingham, Alabama 1956-1963: The Black Struggle for Civil Rights*, all three volumes published in 1989 in Brooklyn by Carlson; Lawrence Reddick, *Crusader Without Violence: A Biography of Martin Luther King, Jr* (1959); Lerone Bennett, *What Manner of Man: A Biography of Martin Luther King, Jr* (1966); William Miller, *Martin Luther King: His Life, Martyrdom and Meaning in the World* (1968); King's own works: *Stride To Freedom: The Montgomery Story* (1958); *Why We Can't Wait* (1964); *Where Do We Go From Here? Chaos or Community?* (1967); Taylor Branch, *Parting the Waters: America in the King Years, 1954-1963* (1988) and *Pillar of Fire: America in the King Years, 1963-1965* (1998); Richard Lischer, *The Preacher King: Martin Luther King, Jr and the Word that Moved America* (1995); Peter Ling, 'Local Leadership in the Early civil rights movement: The South Carolina Citizenship Education Programs of the Highlander Folk School' in *Journal of American Studies*, 29:pp.399-422; and *Martin Luther King, Jr* (2002); James H. Cone, *Martin & Malcolm and America: A Dream or A Nightmare* (1993); Clayborne Carson, *In Struggle:*

SNCC and Black Awakening of the 1960s (1981); *The Autobiography of Martin Luther King, Jr* (1998). See also Carson et al eds:, *A Knock at Midnight: The Great Sermons of Martin Luther King, Jr* (1998); *The Papers of Martin Luther King, Jr*, Vols.1-1V (Berkeley: University of California Press, 1991, 1992, 1996, 2000); B Ward and T. Badger (eds), *The Making of Martin Luther King and the Civil Rights Movement* (1996); M E Dyson: *I May Not Get There With You: The True Martin Luther King, Jr* (2000)

There are also a number of more personalised accounts including: Ralph Abernathy, *And the Walls Come Tumbling Down* (1989); Martin Luther King, Sr. (with Clayton Riley), *Daddy King: An Autobiography* (1980); Coretta Scott King, *My Life With Martin Luther King, Jr.* (1993); Roy Wilkins, *Standing Fast: The Autobiography of Roy Wilkins* (1984); Walter White, *A Man Called White: The Autobiography of Walter White* (1949); Andrew Young, *An Easy Burden: The Civil Rights Movement and the Transformation of America* (1996); John Lewis, *Walking With the Wind: A Memoir of the Movement* (1998); Benjamin Mays, *Born To Rebel: An Autobiography* (1987); N.J. Weiss, *Whitney M. Young and the Struggle for Civil Rights* (1989); Carl Brauer, *John F. Kennedy and the Second Reconstruction* (1977); Mark Stern, *Calculating Visions: Kennedy, Johnson and Civil Rights* (1987); Harvard Sitkoff, *The Struggle for Black Equality* (1993); Hugh Graham, *The Civil Rights Era: Origins and Development of National Policy, 1960-1972* (1990); William B Huie, *He Slew the Dreamer: My Search with James Earl Ray for the Truth About Martin Luther King, Jr* (1997); James Earl Ray, *Who Killed Martin Luther King, Jr? The True Story by the Alleged Assassin* (1997); Adam Fairclough, *To Redeem the Soul of America: The SCLC and Martin Luther King, Jr* (1987, 2001) and *Martin Luther King, Jr*, (1995).

King's intellectual and spiritual development received careful attention in Hanes Walton, Jr, *The Political Philosophy of Martin Luther King, Jr.* (1971) and in John G Ansboro, *Martin Luther King, Jr: The Making of a Mind* (1982); Richard Deats, *Martin Luther King, Jr: Spirit-led Prophet.*

King's intellectual development is also dealt with in the following articles: John E Rathbun, 'Martin Luther King: *The Theology of Social Action*', *Atlantic Quarterly,* 20 (1968), pp.38-53; Warren E Steinkraus, 'Martin Luther King's Personalism and Nonviolence', *Journal of the History of Ideas* 34 (1973), pp.97-111; and Mohan Lal Sharma, 'Martin Luther King: Modern America's Greatest Theologian of Social Action', *Journal of Negro History*, 53 (1968), pp.257-63.

Picture Sources

The author and publishers wish to express their thanks to the following sources of illustrative material and/or permission to reproduce it. They will make proper acknowledgements in future editions in the event that any omissions have occurred.

Getty Images: pp. i, iii, 4, 29, 39, 45, 47, 61, 65, 70, 82, 85, 94, 103, 110, 117. Topham Picturepoint: p.96.

Index

Abernathy, Juanita 44
Abernathy, Rev Ralph 30, 42, 50, 59, 71, 119–21
   Albany movement 68
   arrests and imprisonment 35, 38, 73, 76
ACMHR *see* Alabama Christian Movement for Human Rights
African-Americans
   see also National Association for the Advancement of Coloured People
   and Civil Rights Act 90
   emancipation 1
   poverty 54, 108
   racial justice 12, 43, 48, 75, 112–13
   segregation 2, 3
   unemployment 116
Alabama bus boycott 29–42
Alabama Christian Movement for Human Rights 26–7, 69
Albany movement 65–8
Anderson, W.G. 65–6
Atlanta
   Ebenezer Baptist Church 3, 13, 58
   Morehouse College 3, 11–13, 49

Baez, Joan 104
Baker, Ella 60, 119
Baptist churches 25–6
Barbour, Pius 17
Bates College, Lewiston 12
Belafonte, Harry 71–2, 104

Bennett, Tony 104
Bernstein, Leonard 104
Bertocci, Peter 20
Bevel, James 80, 108
Birmingham Campaign 68–76
Birmingham Sixteenth Street Baptist Church 85
black Muslims 97
black nationalist movements 81
Black Power 46, 81, 98–100, 111–13
bombings 37, 44–5, 85
Boutwell, Alfred 70–1
Bradley, Ms 9
Brandt, Mayor Willy 96
Brightman, Dr Edgar 20
Brown, Rap 81
bus segregation 29–42
   law against 44, 64

Campaign Against Racial Discrimination 95
CARD *see* Campaign Against Racial Discrimination
Carmichael, Stokely 81, 99, 110–12, *110*
Carter, Judge Eugene 40
Chicago riots 107–10
civil disobedience 11
civil rights 14, 58, 63, 90–1, 103
   Birmingham protest 70–1, 78
Civil Rights Act 60, 88–90
Community on the Move for Equality 116

Connor, Eugene 'Bull' 69–70, 72, 77
CORE 60, 64, 81
Curry, Izola 50

Daniel, Alfred 23
Davis Jnr, Sammy 104
Davis, Ossie 104
De Wolf, L.Harold 20, 23
Deats, Richard 104
Democratic Party 92–3
DuBois, W.E.B. 26, 55–6

emancipation from slavery 1

Fairclough, Adam 55
Farmer, James 64, 81
Fellowship of Reconciliation 35, 50
FOR *see* Fellowship of Reconciliation
Forman, James 81
Freedom March 110, 111
Freedom Riders 64, 66

Gandhi, Mahatma 53
    death 15, 55
    non-violent resistance 11, 18, 33, 53
Garrow, David 116
Gaston Motel 70, 78
Ghana independence 46
Goldwater, Senator Barry 91
Great Depression 1
Greenwood 111

Humphrey, Hubert 102

India 52–4
    untouchables 54

Jackson, Jesse 109
'Jim Crow' 3
Johnson, Dr Mordecai 18
Johnson, Lyndon 87, 89–90, 101, 103–4, 106, 108

Kelsey, Professor George 13, 14
Kennedy, Senator John F. 61–3, *61*, 67, 78–9, 85–6, 103
    Civil Rights Act 60
    death 87
Kennedy, Senator Robert 63, 78
King, Alberta (mother of MLK) 3, 5
King, Alfred Daniel (brother of MLK) 2, 78
King, Bernice Albertine (daughter of MLK) 69, 116
King, Christine (sister of MLK) 2
King, Coretta Scott (wife of MLK) 47, 65, 70, *121*
    India trip 52
    marriage 21–3, 35, 38, 65, 117
King, Dexter (son of MLK) 67
King, Martin Luther, *39*, *45*, 47, 65, *82*, *85*, *94*, *110*
    CIVIL RIGHTS ACTIVITIES
        arrests and imprisonment 35, 60, 62–3, 66–8, 73, 76
        attacked 50
        bus boycott 30–7
        court appearances 40–1
        death plot 92
        and Kennedy 61, 79, 85
        leadership qualities 56–7, 65, 68
        letter from jail 72–3
        and Malcolm X 98–9
        Nobel Peace Prize 93, 95–7
        non-violence 33–5, 37, 40
        right to vote 49
        temperament 45
        trip to India 52–4
        world recognition 93, 95–7
    EARLY LIFE
        birth 1, 6
        bus experience 9
        civil disobedience 11
        death of grandmother 7

family relationships 4–5
friendship with white boy 7
hatred of white people 8
influence of father 3–5
EDUCATION
  Booker T. Washington High
    School 9
  Boston University 20–8
  Crozer Seminary 15–17
  Morehouse College 13–14
MINISTRY 13, 24
  against capitalism 13, 16–17
  Dexter Avenue Baptist Church
    24–5, 58
  influences 14–16
  opposition to communism
    16–17
  preaching 16, 22, 122
  relationship with Church 6–7,
    12–15, 119
PUBLICATIONS
  Jail Diary 67
  Stride to Freedom 50
SERMONS 27
  'A Tender Heart and a Tough
    Mind' 67
  Gandhi 54–5
  'Love in Action' 68
  'Loving Your Enemeies' 68
  'Three Dimensions of a
    Complete Life' 24, 95
SPEECHES
  'I have a dream' 83–5
  'The Negro and the
    Constitution' 10
DEATH 120–2
  eulogy at funeral 12
  funeral 70, 71, 119
King, Martin Luther III (son of
  MLK) 67
King, Martin Luther Snr
  (father of MLK) 2–3, 4, 23, 25

  civil rights 3–4, 8, 14, 67
  family relationships 4–5, 38
  leader of Atlanta black com-
    munity 14
King Rally, Washington 82
King, Yolanda Denise (daughter of
  MLK) 27, 67
Ku Klux Klan 2, 88, 97

Lawson, Rev James M. 50, 59
Levison 57
Lewis, James 81
Lewis, John 103
Lewis, Rufus 26
Little, Malcolm *see* Malcolm X
lynchings 2

McKissick, Floyd 112
Malcolm X 97–9
March on Washington 80–3
*Martin Luther King and the Montgomery
  Story* 50
Marx, Karl
  Communist Manifesto 16
  Das Capital 16
Mays, Benjamin Elijah 12–14, 49
Memphis 116, 119
  Mason Temple 120
Meredith, James 110
Ming and Delaney 61
Mississippi Freedom Domocratic
  Party 92
Mississippi Freedom Summer 90
Montgomery
  bus protest 29–42
  Dexter Avenue Baptist Church
    24–6, 58
  Holt Street Baptist Church 31
  Montgomery Improvement
    Association 31–4
  non-violent resistance 34
Moore, Rev Douglas E. 59

INDEX   149

Morehouse College 3, 11–13, 49
Morgan, Juliette 33
Muhammad, Elijah, Muslim movement 81

NAACP, *see* National Association for the Advancement of Coloured People
Nation of Islam 81, 97
National Association for the Advancement of Coloured People 3, 14, 26–7
  non-violent resistance 33–4
Negro revolution of 1963, 89, 91
Negro schools and colleges 2
Nehru, Jawaharlal 52
Newton, Huey P. 81
Niebuhr, Reinhold 'Moral Man and Immoral Society' 16
Nixon, E.D. 30, 38
Nixon, Richard 62, 63
Nkrumah, Kwame 46–7
non-violent resistance 11, 33–42, 53, 107
  'How to Practice Nonviolence' 50
  'The Power of Nonviolence' 50
North Carolina A and T College 58

Operation Breadbasket 109

Pan Africa movement 56
Parks, Rosa 29–32, *29*
Paul VI, Pope 96
Peter, Paul and Mary 104
police brutality 102–3
Poor People's Campaign 115–17, 119
Powell, Mary 21, 23
Prayer Pilgrimage 49

race riots 2, 91, 107
racial bias
  on buses 8, 29
  in housing 20
racial justice 12
racial pride 98, 112
Rauschenbusch, Walter, 'Christianity and the Social Crisis' 15–16
Republican Party 1, 92–3
Rice, Thomas 'Daddy' 3
right to vote 49
Robeson, Paul 55
Robinson, Jo Ann 26
Rustin, Bayard 57

St. Augustine, Florida 88
SCLC *see* Southern Christian Leadership Conference
Scott, Coretta, *see* Coretta Scott King
segregation in the South 2, 3, 8–9, 66, 105
  'Jim Crow' 3
  legislation 80
  poverty of black people 10, 54, 108
  in public schools 49, 56, 69
  and small children 5
Selma March 102–6, *102*
Shuttlesworth, Rev Fred 69, 71
sit-ins 58–9, 62, 64
Smiley, Glen 35, 42, 50
SNCC *see* Student Nonviolent Coordinating Committee
Southern Christian Leadership Conference 44–5, 58, 69, 81, 107–8
  Albany movement 66
  internal disagreements 117
Southern states
  changing political structure 92
  discrimination 5
  segregation 2, 3
student activists 58–60
Student Nonviolent Coordinating Committee 60, 111

Thoreau, Henry David, 'On Civil
    Disobedience' 11
Thurman, Howard 20
Truman, Harry S. 15

untouchables 54

Vietnam war 114–15
voting rights 49, 90, 101–5
Voting Rights Act 101, 103, 106

Wallace, Governor George 69, 102, 105

Washington, Booker T. 56
    'Atlanta Compromise' 14
Watts riots 107
Whitaker, Ed 17
white supremacist system 2
Williams, Alberta, *see* Alberta King
    (mother of MLK)
Williams, Rev A.D. (grandfather of
    MLK) 3, 5
Women's Political Council 30

Young, Andrew 119